M000033634

All in 4 God

Devotions
for Young
Women

Megan Clinton

Author of *Smart Girls, Smart Choices*

HARVEST HOUSE PUBLISHERS
EUGENE, OREGON

Cover by Koechel Peterson & Associates, Inc. Minneapolis, Minnesota

Megan Clinton is represented by Thomas J. Winters & King, Inc., Tulsa, Oklahoma

Formerly titled *Totally God's 4 Life Devotional.*

All emphasis in Scripture quotations is added by the author.

ALL IN 4 GOD
Copyright © 2009 by Megan Clinton
Published by Harvest House Publishers
Eugene, Oregon 97402
www.harvesthousepublishers.com

ISBN 978-0-7369-4724-4 (pbk.)
ISBN 978-0-7369-4725-1 (eBook)

Printed in China

12 13 14 15 16 17 / FC-CD / 10 9 8 7 6 5 4 3 2 1

Acknowledgments

I am a little pencil in the hand of a writing God
who is sending a love letter to the world.
MOTHER TERESA

I love this quote. My mom used it in a book, and I wanted to use it too. It reminds me of how small we are compared to the large and majestic God who loves us so much. And how He uses each of us in different roles to carry out His message of love to the world.

A special thank you to Laree Lindburg for your willingness to help me with this devotional. Your time and wisdom are so much appreciated.

Kudos to Harvest House Publishers for your support and dedication. In particular to Terry Glaspey, Carolyn McCready, and Gene Skinner for providing a special platform to reach young women all across America.

To Joshua Straub, Amy Feigel, and Laura Faidley for your editing, writing, research, and insight—you guys are a great help!

And to my parents. I love you both so much and wouldn't be where I am today without your faithful prayers and love for me. I can write a devotional only because of your faithfulness and commitment to raise me with the love of God. You have been living examples of what it means to be all in for God!

Contents

Introduction

I've been thinking about you a lot lately—yes, really.

I have tried to imagine what you look like, how you feel about yourself, and where you live. Mostly I have been wondering about what's been on your heart lately. The stuff you think about when no one else is around.

Have you ever wondered at times about God—who He is, whether He really knows you and loves you, how He wants you to respond to difficult life situations, and if He is disappointed in you or simply there for you?

When you listen to people speak about God and life, everyone has an opinion, but real answers seem hard to come by.

As you read, I want you to know that God loves you, and I believe He has a dream for your life. The Bible even says He is wild about you. I really like that. I wrote this devotional because I want you to know that regardless of the situation you find yourself in,

God is there in the middle of it all and promises to see you through.

As for me, I am just crazy enough to believe that if you will search and reach for Him, if you will press in close to Him, you will find Him, and He will be your rock, your strong tower.

Warmly,

1

WHO IS GOD?

Devotions to help us better understand who He is

Above All Names

God said to Moses, "I AM WHO I AM. This is what you
are to say to the Israelites: I AM has sent me to you."

EXODUS 3:14

Did you know that the Bible includes more than 100 names for God? And that doesn't even count the variations to these names! Whew!

Another bit of trivia—How many words do you think are in the English language?

> 50,000?
> 75,000?
> 100,000?

Try 171, 476! Plus another 47,156 words we don't really use. That's getting close to a quarter of a million words in the English language! But out of all the words in the English language, one will always stand out above all the rest: *God*!

Let's take a look at a few of the many names of our one God:

Jehovah—I Am. One who always exists, eternal and unchangeable.

El-Shaddai—God Almighty

Adonai—Lord, our master and owner

Jehovah-jireh—Jehovah will provide

Jehovah-rophe—Jehovah heals

Jehovah-nissi—Jehovah, my banner

Jehovah-M'Kaddesh—Jehovah, who sanctifies (forgives)

Jehovah-shalom—Jehovah, our peace

Jehovah-tsidekenu—Jehovah, our righteousness

Jehovah-rohi—Jehovah, my Shepherd

Jehovah-shammah—Jehovah is there

By learning the names of God, we get to know a little more about His character. Studying the original usage of God's names is helpful because today the words *God* or *Lord* mean simply "supreme being" or "sovereign of the universe." That's great, but God is so much more!

I don't know about you, but reading the names of God gives me joy! When I am scared, thinking about the names *Jehovah-shalom* and *Jehovah-shammah* makes me feel safe. When I'm worried or nervous, the names *Jehovah-jireh* and *Jehovah-rohi* remind me of God's care.

When my heart is broken or a family member has a terrible illness, the name *Jehovah-rophe* reassures me that regardless of what happens, God will heal in the way He thinks is best. And during crazy, unpredictable times in our world, just the name *Jehovah* fills me with comfort. He has always existed, He is eternal, and He is unchangeable. I love that, especially when something major seems to be shifting in our world every day. God doesn't budge.

His love for us does not change either, and that is very cool. Even when we are unfaithful to Him, He will stay faithful to His word—and to us.

By calling Himself *I Am*, God assures us that He has always been. He is righteousness, peace, our Shepherd, the one who is there. He's the King of kings and Lord of lords. He is our Prince of Peace, our Mighty God and Everlasting Father. His name is above all names—that's our God!

What's a Girl to Do?

Try to use God's names in your everyday life, like when you pray. The names are straight from the Bible, so you can use them to talk to God. When you think of the Lord or talk about Him, remember these descriptions of who He is. They will not only help you in tough times but also help others as well. I challenge you to pray using another one of God's names this week.

All in with God

Father, thank You for giving me Your names. Now that I have read these titles, I feel I know You even better. Help me to understand more and more aspects of Your character, Lord. I love You and trust You. In Jesus' name, amen.

Step One

For God so loved the world that He gave His
only begotten Son, that whoever believes in
Him shall not perish, but have eternal life.

JOHN 3:16 NASB

I want to share with you the reason I wrote this little book. If you take only one thing from the entire book, please let it be the words in this devotion. I hope they will help you make the most important decision you will ever make on this earth.

In this book I talk about what it's like to live a life with Jesus at the center. I know that may sound weird, but let me explain.

The story of humanity starts with Adam and Eve. The cool part is that God specifically gave them permission to roam freely and to eat from any tree they wanted—except for one. So what did they do? They did as any young child would do when Mom says "Don't eat that lollipop until after you eat your lunch!" They snuck an apple from the tree and ate from it anyway. From this point on a barrier was placed between God and humans. This barrier, called sin, keeps us from truly relating to God. In fact, after Adam and Eve ate from the tree, they felt guilty and ashamed, and they just hid from God. Have you ever felt that way, as if you just wanted to hide? We all have. That's because when Adam and Eve disobeyed God, their sin affected all of humanity. You and I sin every day. Romans 3:23 says, "For all have sinned and fall short of the glory of God."

But the good news is this: God loved us so much that He sent His only Son to die for us so that the barrier would be lifted! And if we confess to God that we are sinners, believe in Him, and make Him the center of our lives, we will have life in heaven.

If you haven't made this step yet, I encourage you to right now. The following prayer is the most important prayer you'll ever pray. And it's the first step toward becoming all in for God.

Pray this prayer from your heart to God's heart:

> *Father, I know I have sinned, and I'm sorry. I am now ready to turn away from my sinful past and start a new life in You. Please forgive me of my sins. I invite Jesus to be my Savior. I want Him to be the center of my life and lead it. Please send Your Holy Spirit to help me obey You and live for You. I pray all this in Jesus' name. Amen.*

If you prayed that prayer, let me be the first to say congratulations! The Bible says that right now, because you prayed that prayer, all of the angels in heaven are rejoicing!

Now it's time to focus on your newfound faith in God!

Your next step, through the power of the Holy Spirit, is to learn more and walk tight with God. Start praying to Him. This requires nothing more than you just talking to Him. Begin with the prayer at the end of this devotion. It is a great start! Read the Bible. Go to church. And find another Christian woman or a group of girls your age you know who can begin to mentor you and help you understand what having Jesus at the center of your life is all about.

I love you and I am praying for you! I trust and hope that you are encouraged and will grow stronger and deeper in your walk with Jesus. Let's journey together and live with Jesus at the center of our lives, all in for Him!

What's a Girl to Do?

If you decided to believe in Jesus for eternal life— celebrate! Your sins are forgiven! Maybe you already knew Jesus, and this was just a nice reminder of your salvation. Or maybe you are not ready. If this is true for you, pray and ask God to speak to you. Ask Him to give you the faith you need to be saved. He will listen. After all, this is the most important decision you'll ever make!

All in with God

Father, thank You for always being there—for listening and for loving me first. I pray that You would prepare my heart to fully understand who You are and what You desire from me as Your follower. I want to know You more! Teach me, Lord. I am so grateful for the free gift of salvation for all who believe in Jesus. I love You. In Jesus' name I pray. Amen.

Created

By faith, we see the world called into existence by God's word, what we see created by what we don't see.

HEBREWS 11:3 MSG

When you were a kid, did you ever ask where the sun, moon, or world came from? I know I did—a lot. But seriously, this question is big. As followers of Jesus, we believe that the Bible is 100 percent true. No ifs, ands, or buts. And the very first sentence of the Bible makes an important statement: *God created.*

So what, Megan? Well, not everybody believes that God created the world. Some people believe we came from monkeys. (Well, maybe my brother did, but not me!) But the Bible says that God created everything. Genesis says that He just spoke the words, and...*poof!* Plants, animals, birds, water, me, you... You name it, and it just appeared. Do you find that hard to grasp?

God's pretty big, huh? But God didn't just create way back when. When you and I were smaller than the period at the end of this sentence, God began to put us together intricately. Fingers, toes, a heart that beats, a brain way more complex than the biggest computer out there, eye color, curly hair or straight hair... Down to the last little detail, God put you together.

Does that blow your mind? It does mine! You are unique, and no other girl in the entire world is quite like you. Just look at your fingerprint. No two persons are the same!

The apostle Paul says that when we look around our world, everything God created shouts out about the best Artist ever (Psalm 19:1). God made everything for His glory—and He's good!

Think about it—gorgeous flowers, snow-capped mountains, breathtaking sunsets, and even you! Everything exists to point back to how awesome and good God is.

But here's the deal. A lot of people don't believe in God. They think that Jesus, God's Son, was just a good man, a wonderful teacher, a prophet. Some people think the Bible is just a silly old book. What do you think? Looking around at the beauty and complexity of creation, it's hard for me to believe that it all just happened by chance.

If we believe that God created us as His girls...well, that's a big deal. It's *huge*! It means that God is our Creator. And if He created us, we belong to Him. My life and your life have just one purpose: to point to Him.

Today, take a minute to stop and think about who

God *really* is. Go for a walk outside and look around you at some of the masterpieces He has created, like the mountains, rivers, lakes, grass, trees... God doesn't just work magic tricks. He *creates*.

What's a Girl to Do?

This is a challenging topic. Many Christians today are being drawn away from the truth that God really did create the world. This is as good a time as any to pray and ask God to help you to understand and believe in who He is. You will be tempted to agree with other points of view under pressure, but stand firm; our God is the One and only, and He will be so pleased at your faith in Him.

All in with God

Father, I live in a time when people doubt Your ability to create all things. All around me, people take the praise for things only You have done. Father, forgive them. Forgive me when I do the same thing. I want to truly understand You as the Creator of all. Help me, Lord, to stand firm for Your truth. In Jesus' name, amen.

A Heart in Hiding

Is there anyplace I can go to avoid your Spirit? to be out of your sight? If I climb to the sky, you're there! If I go underground, you're there.

Psalm 139:7-8 MSG

When I was little, I loved to play hide-and-seek. It was always fun to find a place that was all my own. I usually made Zach, my younger brother, try to find me first. Part of the fun was scaring him to death!

But have you ever done something you *knew* was wrong...and then wanted to run and hide? I have. Way back in the Garden of Eden, Adam and Eve hid from God after they sinned. And ever since then, we have been hiding too.

But do you think we can really hide from God? The Bible says we can't. He's always there—always.

Consider that the Lord has looked at your soul and knows your heart. He watches every move you make. He gets your inner thoughts and evaluates where you're headed in life. Before you say a word, He knows what it'll be. It's amazing how well He knows you. (See Psalm 139:1-4.)

God knows us intimately. He knows our secrets, and yet He loves us. He may not always love our behavior, but He loves us.

Let me help you understand how great His love is for you. King David, who was known as the man after God's own heart, was close to God. And yet look at all the sins David committed.

- He stole another man's wife.

- He got her pregnant.

- He told the commander of his army to put Uriah (the woman's husband) in the front line and then fall back so he would be killed.

Wait a minute! David, a man who loved God, was an adulterer *and* a murderer? Yes! He repented of his wrongs, and although God forgave him, David still had to endure some harsh consequences for his sin, just as we all do. But he also knew, without a doubt, God's intimate love for him.

God doesn't give up on us when we mess up. Not a chance! The Bible says that God is changing us from the inside out. And what God starts, He always finishes.

Ask God today to help you be a woman after God's own heart.

What's a Girl to Do?

The only way we will know how much God loves us is to read the Bible. Pray and ask God to show you His love for you and to make that love real in your heart. Trust in Him and go far for Him because of how far He has gone for you.

All in with God

Father, I can be so concerned about whom I identify with in this life. Friends, clubs, colleges, music, clothes...the temptation to fit in is everywhere. But what is truly important is identifying with You. I want to know You more, Lord. I want to understand how far You have gone and will go for me, and I want to grow in how far I will go for You. In Jesus' name, amen.

Not a Deadbeat Dad

A father to the fatherless, a defender of the
widows, is God in his holy dwelling.
PSALM 68:5

A few years ago, I went to the Dominican Republic
with my dad to visit a girl we sponsor through
World Vision. She was so excited to see us, and I was
just as happy to see her!

My eyes were opened like never before. I saw poverty,
illness, crime, and so much more. I received a much-
needed wake-up call about how many blessings I enjoy:
a home, a family, a church, food and clothes...The list
could go on and on!

You may have noticed I counted family as a blessing.
But I know you may live in a family that has serious
struggles. Your parents may be divorced, one parent
could be absent, or maybe your mom or dad has died.
Perhaps you were adopted or are in foster care. There are
a lot of reasons why our parents may not be around—
especially our dads.

When I looked into this, I found that America is

filled with fatherless kids. The statistics I found were astounding:

- Up to 50 percent of former foster kids or probation youth become homeless within the first 18 months of emancipation.
- Youth in foster care are 44 percent less likely to graduate from high school, and after emancipation, 40 to 50 percent never complete high school.
- Girls in foster care are 60 percent more likely to give birth before age 21.
- Forty percent of American kids will wake up in a home tomorrow where their biological fathers do not live.

Fatherless homes add some alarming stats too! They account for 63 percent of youth suicides, 90 percent of homeless and runway children, 71 percent of high school dropouts, 85 percent of youths in prison, and 59 percent of teen mothers.

Even if you have a father, he may not always be around. He may be deployed in the military, working around the clock, or just plain busy. I know that my dad will not be able to be my "everything." That is a job only God can do. A dad's hugs mean so much to a girl's life, but only God can meet the deepest longings inside her. And He is a Father for all.

Take comfort in His promise. Take refuge in His arms. I pray that regardless of your family situation, God will be the Father you have always wanted and the Father you need. He loves you, and if you know Him as your Lord and Savior, you are a daughter of the King. Ask Him to be your Daddy today!

What's a Girl to Do?

If you are fatherless, have hope—you have a perfect Father! God is your Father for all time. Lean on that truth. We will always have a Father whose arms are open wide!

All in with God

Father, I didn't realize just how true that title is. You are my Father forever. Thank You, Lord. And You are not only my Father but also my Savior and so much more. I love You. Be extra close to those who struggle with the loss of a parent, and comfort them. In Jesus' name, amen.

Surrender

*Delight yourself in the LORD and he will
give you the desires of your heart.*

PSALM 37:4

I just love this verse, don't you? My desires—hmmm,
let's see! A boyfriend who's tall and well-built with
brown hair like Zac Efron. A luxury car, like a brand-new
white convertible Mercedes-Benz. A beautiful home on
the beach with a cascading eternity pool in the back-
yard! Yeah! Okay...maybe that's not what this verse is
referring to. (But a girl's gotta dream right?)

The first part of this verse is the real key. "Delight
yourself in the LORD." When we truly put the Lord
first, His desires become ours. Now let's talk about what
that means.

As Christians we often struggle with what following the Lord actually entails. At first thought, I imagine
following the Lord means going to a far-off country
with no running water, lots of bugs, and nasty things
to eat. In no way is that a put-down. It takes a special
calling and a unique person to serve God as a missionary.

What do you imagine when you think of a life totally surrendered to Jesus?

Anyone can commit her way to the Lord, regardless of her age or what she is doing in life. We often think we need to move to a special place for God to use us in His work. The truth is that all of us can become tools for God right where He has placed us. In school, at work, on the court, in the field, in practice, at the bus stop, at home... God wants to use us everywhere to minister to those He loves. And He tells us that He'll bless us for being available. If we trust in Him and do good, and if we delight in Him, He promises to give us the desires of our heart. God asks us to commit our ways to Him. When you do, "He will make your righteousness shine like the dawn, the justice of your cause like the noonday sun" (Psalm 37:3-6).

Isn't that awesome? Does this apply for us today? You bet! It totally does. If God sees that we trust in Him and long to do His will, He will bless us.

Here is one warning: God is *not* a genie in a bottle. If you think, *I'll just do as He says so I can get whatever I want*, guess again. It doesn't work that way. God knows our hearts. He sees us truly delight in Him, trust Him, and do good things for Him. We can't trick God into blessing us.

Let's pray and ask God to give us a heart that longs to serve Him as He desires. Let's take our selfish desires out of the equation. Throw our wants aside. When we have done so, God will open our eyes and show us His goodness and His ways. And that will be all the blessing we will ever need!

What's a Girl to Do?

I know this is a tall order, but let's not get discouraged and down about all that God asks of us. Just take it one step at a time. The first thing may be to pray or to deny some of our wants. Maybe you need to work on trusting in Him. He really does want to give you the desires of your heart!

All in with God

Father, I want to know You more. Please plant within my heart the seed to do Your will, trust in You, do good, and delight in You. I know that when I am fully living for You, the desires I have will already be filled—with You! I believe that having Your joy in my life is a huge blessing. I love You! In Jesus' name, amen.

Getting Some Alone Time

*Behold, the LORD was passing by! And a great and
strong wind was rending the mountains and breaking in
pieces the rocks before the LORD; but the LORD was not
in the wind. And after the wind an earthquake, but the
LORD was not in the earthquake. After the earthquake
a fire, but the LORD was not in the fire; and after the fire
a sound of a gentle blowing...And behold, a voice came
to him and said, "What are you doing here, Elijah?"*

1 KINGS 19:11-13 NASB

New York City! One of my most favorite places to
visit. Saks, Macy's, H&M, Nordstrom, Banana
Republic...all in one location (even if I can't afford to
buy anything)!

The only bummer is the constant sounds of city
life all around. Police sirens, car horns, construction
machinery, truck engines...after a while, I need to get
away to a nearby park and separate myself from all the
fury. There, I can hear the wind in the trees rustling the
leaves and birds chirping in the warm air. Ahh...peace.

I agree with 1 Kings 19. We can sense God's presence

in the gentle whisper of a breeze, the soft snore of a newborn baby, the cheep-cheep of fluffy yellow chicks, and the swooshing of sand beneath our feet on the beach. In the quiet moments of our hearts we hear God best.

God is everywhere. The theological term for this is *omnipresent*. Always around. Even when the police sirens pass by, machines pound on concrete, or annoyed people blast their car horns, God is there.

But quiet is hard to come by in this day and age. We'd have to turn off our cell phones, iPods, televisions, and computers. We'd have to leave the city, get away from all the cars, and turn from tons of people. But then again, maybe we just need to go on a walk in the park with our dog or go to our room and shut the door.

Whatever we do, being quiet and listening to God is a choice. There is just something special about being alone and listening for God. It's intimate. He knows it, and we feel it.

Choosing to distance yourself from distractions like phones, computers, and the TV can be difficult and could make you look...well, funny to your friends. But the benefits of alone time with God are incredible. Knowing that the Creator of the universe wants to spend time with you, talk with you, and hear your thoughts and concerns—is anything better than that?

He knows your heart. He knows your future. He knows your fears. He knows your failures—and He loves you anyway. God already knew what Elijah was doing on that mountain, but still He asked. That's how God works! He wants a relationship. Communication. He wants to hear what we have to say even though He already knows our thoughts. He wants you to see Him in the gentle blowing of the wind. He wants to be the sole owner of your heart.

But the choice is yours. Choose to listen. Find a quiet place and meet with Him. Be still and embrace His presence.

What's a Girl to Do?

Getting away from all the distractions in life is hard. We may be able to escape outward things, but shutting off our minds is another task. I find that prayer helps. If I pray or read the Bible, my mind wanders to the things of God and not the world. Try getting away to a quiet place sometime this week and read, pray, and listen. It works for me.

All in with God

Father, You do love me and have called me to be all in for You. I want to be all Yours, Lord, but I struggle to know what that looks like or how to do it exactly. Teach me Your ways. Open my mind to You during the quiet times so I can know Your voice even in the loud times. I love You, God. In Jesus' name, amen.

Rebellion

My son, do not make light of the Lord's discipline,
and do not lose heart when he rebukes you,
because the Lord disciplines those he loves, and
he punishes everyone he accepts as a son.

HEBREWS 12:5-6

My dad and I are close. We share a special father-daughter relationship. When I needed discipline, Dad administered it—not to make my life miserable, but because he loved me. He didn't do it because he was angry at me. This is why I respect him and why we have such a good bond today. Learning from the way he disciplined me has taught me how I want to discipline my own kids someday.

Parents have a tough job. When God gives them a child, they soon realize the extent of the responsibility. This babe can't do anything for himself. Days and nights are spent on the baby's care. But a baby's mistakes are innocent. An infant can't discern danger from safety or right from wrong.

You and I have pretty much outgrown the days of

time-outs. But regardless of what age we are, we still experience consequences for our choices. Your mom or dad may not be the one you end up giving account to. It could be a teacher, police officer, or judge.

If you often disobey authority and rebel against control, think about this: Are you rebelling against God as well? I totally understand that you may not have parents who have disciplined you lovingly. You may have even been abused or neglected. And for that, I am terribly sorry. God does not discipline with anger when we mess up or totally defy Him in some way. Rather, He does it because He wants what is best for us. His will is good and acceptable and perfect (Romans 12:2 NASB).

Hebrews 12 encourages us to not brush aside the Lord's discipline. We are to stay positive and not lose heart, because God loves us. He punishes everyone He accepts as sons and daughters (see Hebrews 12:6). In our day, when kids can sue their parents or "divorce" their family, this Bible passage may be difficult to accept. But God's Word is truth.

Whether we have had good parents or bad, God truly loves us, and His discipline is for our own good. He loves us enough to correct our behavior so we will lead lives that please Him.

What's a Girl to Do?

Maybe this devotion has caught you rebelling against

those who discipline you. Maybe you have had horrible experiences with discipline. Those don't represent who God is. Open your heart today to the truth: God is love (1 John 4:8).

All in with God

Father, You love me with an everlasting love. I understand that Your discipline is for my good because I am Your child. The way the world sees discipline is so different from the way Your Word describes it. I want to obey You and not rebel. Guide me closer to Your will so that when Your discipline comes, I will accept it and appreciate the love that motivates it. In Jesus' name, amen.

THE REAL ME

Devotions to encourage us to be real in Christ

Perfume of Heaven

*Your very lives are a letter that anyone can read
just by looking at you. Christ himself wrote it—
not with ink, but with God's living Spirit; not
chiseled into stone, but carved into human lives.*

2 CORINTHIANS 3:2-3 MSG

Texting, Twitter, Facebook—in today's world, connecting is super easy. I love talking to my friends, staying in touch with my family, and just looking at pictures of everybody. But sometimes, I can get lost in the craziness and forget who I am.

Who am I apart from my friends, my schoolwork, my family, and my youth group? Who is the real me? The real you?

The media tell us some pretty crazy things about how we should think, feel, and act. I love clothes as much as the next person, but too often we're led to believe that unless we sport the latest from Hollister and American Eagle or look just like the girls in *Seventeen* and *Teen Vogue*, we're slacking in the looks department.

But stop and think about it. Who defines you? Fashions change, and models get old. But fortunately, God's Word doesn't. My mom always told me, "You may be the only Bible some of your friends will ever read." The apostle Paul even wrote that we are human letters from God that communicate His glory to the world around us. This means that God often uses you and me to get His message of love to other people. I love that! But it makes me wonder, *Am I living in a way that lets God communicate to others through my life?*

Who are we? We are God's text messages to the world: "I love you," "I've saved you," "You matter to God," "Don't give up hope," "I am here."

Here are some word pictures the Bible uses to describe who we are:

- a chosen people—God's daughters
- a royal priesthood—princesses in God's royal court
- God's own possession—His own treasure (1 Peter 2:9)
- shining stars—set apart in the darkness of this world (Philippians 2:15)
- a sweet aroma of the knowledge of Christ—God's perfume (2 Corinthians 2:14)

That's a pretty amazing list, and it's easy for me to look at it and think, *I'm never gonna measure up to that. I'm just an ordinary girl!* Maybe you're thinking the same thing. But God doesn't wait for us to get our act together before He speaks these words over us.

Right now, regardless of what you've done, if you have trusted in Jesus as your Savior, you are His daughter. You are His princess. You are His treasure. You are His perfume. God's Word says so!

And here's the best part: None of it depends on us. God declares these things about us. The labels we receive from the world every day are usually bogus and hurtful, but the titles God has given us show us who we really are. Our identity depends on our hearts, not our hairdos.

Take some time today to dig into the rich treasure chest of the Bible and discover something new about who you really are.

Being popular can't even compare.

What's a Girl to Do?

When times get tough, remember all the wonderful names God has for you. You really are special to Him. Let's embrace these truth-filled titles and live out our identity in Christ for all people to know and read.

All in with God

Father, open my eyes so I may see the truth of who I am in You. Satan wants me to forget how beautiful and lovely I am in You. Lord, help me to be strong and boldly display the letter of Christ, which is written on my heart. In Jesus' name, amen.

Crazy for You

Food for the stomach and the stomach for food.

1 CORINTHIANS 6:13

Chubby, unattractive, unathletic—do any of these labels sound familiar? Our obsession with being fit or thin didn't start yesterday. Maybe you were called hurtful names as a child, or maybe your parents pushed you to be skinny.

Or maybe your older sister, who is a size two, got all the attention. Perhaps you're trying to get the attention of your perfect guy. You might even be trying to control your diet in unhealthy ways in an otherwise out-of-control world.

Every day, I see girls who struggle with their weight. Hey, it's a battle for me too! No girl on this planet, regardless of how godly she is, is immune from the insecurity that comes with trying to be picture-perfect. I struggled to keep the infamous "freshman 15" off this year.

It's rough being a girl who is growing into a woman. A million and one different things are going on in our bodies. And a lot of times, we're way too hard on ourselves. But be honest—no two bodies are alike. Each of us was uniquely put together by God (Psalm 139:13). And yet we swear there must be a perfect figure.

"All I want is to be size..."

"I'll be happy if I weigh..."

"Everyone will like me when I look like..."

We talk like this all the time. And somehow, we tend to think that hitting a certain weight or jeans size will make us happy. But it's all lies.

Can we honestly say with the psalmist, "I praise you, for I am fearfully and wonderfully made" (Psalm 139:14 ESV)? Do we really believe that about our bodies?

One of my friends who struggles with bulimia told me, "I can't stop. I don't know what to do...I eat, but all I can think about is getting the food out of me so I won't get fat."

An actress named Tracy Gold had an eating disorder too. Here's how she describes it:

> It's a statement of not loving yourself. Your whole world is consumed with how people perceive you and what they're thinking about you. But you can never change what people are going to say about you and think about you. You have to know how you feel about yourself inside.

If you want to beat the labels, you've got to know the truth about yourself—about who God says you are. Spend time memorizing Psalm 139. Allow these truths to sink into your being. Then every time a negative thought about the way you look comes into your mind, you can beat it with the truth!

The Bible says that Jesus is crazy about you. He's so happy, He bursts out in song! (See Zephaniah 3:17.) To be all in for God means giving Jesus complete control of your life—even your diet.

Do you need to peel off some labels today that are actually lies? God's label for you is the best of all: "This is My girl, and I love her." And the best part? It's true.

What's a Girl to Do?

Ask yourself, *Do I believe I am worth fighting for?* That is the real question. Girls die from trying to control their eating. Satan uses this as a tactic to control us. It's all a game—let's sit this one out.

All in with God

Father, I have not loved myself as You tell me to. You are faithful and worthy of praise. You have made me in Your image. Forgive me, Lord. Help me to beat my obsession with looks and weight. In Jesus' name, amen.

Identity Theft

*Set your mind on the things above, not
on the things that are on earth.*
COLOSSIANS 3:2 NASB

A lot of nights alone in bed, I think about being loved, cherished, held. I want somebody to share my life with, to know me—the real me. You too?

My dad often tells me how much he loves me and God loves me. To be honest, I have often struggled with the God part—that He really loves me. I mean, come on. I constantly fall short of who God wants me to be and what He wants me to do. And then I wonder, *How could He love me?*

I believe most girls I know feel the same way and have trouble believing that God really loves them. They may say God loves them, but they do unhealthy things in order to feel loved. Let me explain.

I see girls pursue guys at any cost. They turn their backs on their girlfriends, give up activities they once enjoyed, listen over and over to sappy love songs on their iPods, and daydream about their princes. Many young women are filling themselves with anything to feel loved, ultimately losing their sense of self and their identity. But I want you to know this: Our identity in Christ is secure.

Let me show you what Jesus did. He starts a conversation with Peter that goes something like this: "Look, you are going to deny Me three times before the rooster crows."

Peter says something like, "No way. Even if I have to die with You, I will not deny You" (see Matthew 26:34-35).

Be careful what you say, because pride can often make us put our foot in our mouths. And Peter did just that. After Jesus was taken into the custody of the Jewish leaders to be prosecuted and crucified, Peter did deny Jesus—three times. Afterward, he felt so horrible that he wept bitterly. I'll bet Peter thought he'd lost his identity in Christ.

Here is the amazing part. After Jesus rose from the grave, Mary Magdalene and Mary the mother of James visited Jesus' burial site to anoint Him with spices. When they entered the tomb, a young man wearing a white robe told them that Jesus had risen from the dead. But the point here is this: When he told them the good news that Jesus had risen, he specifically said, "Go tell Jesus' disciples *and Peter*" (Mark 16:5-7).

Did you see what Jesus did? He instructed the angel

to personally send a shout-out to Peter so Peter would know that Jesus forgave him.

When I struggle to know that God loves me, I remind myself of Peter. And then I start looking for the "little hugs" God places in my life.

He does the same for you, often through other people: messengers who show you how much God loves you, the encouraging words of a friend, a kind gesture by a stranger, a sweet text message from your mom. Your identity is secure in His love for you. Look for it today.

What's a Girl to Do?

Make an effort this week to consciously focus on God's Word and reminders of His love for you. Look up verses and choose to let Him show you your true identity. When you do, the world's temptations will seem to fade.

All in with God

Father, thank You for loving me and helping me know who I am in You. I fall so easily and tend to focus my eyes on things that bring me down. Help me to fix my eyes on You so my identity is secure in You. In Jesus' name, amen.

Rescued

By grace you have been saved through faith; and
that not of yourselves, it is the gift of God; not as
a result of works, so that no one may boast.
EPHESIANS 2:8-9 NASB

As a little girl, I loved to dream of a handsome prince coming to my rescue. In my play world, Ken always fought off the bad guys to keep Barbie safe. I watched *Sleeping Beauty* and *Cinderella* a lot, oftentimes with the secret hope that I too would one day meet my own perfect prince.

But despite Disney's dreamy depictions, I have found that life isn't so predictable and rosy. Even Cinderella and Princess Aurora (who have super big chests and tiny waists...gotta love those animators) have problems. Both princesses seem to be destined for something great, but both are in danger from would-be destroyers.

So Cinderella has no dress to wear to the ball, and Princess Aurora falls under the spell of Maleficent, the wicked fairy godmother.

Each fairy tale has twists and turns, but at the end of the day, only one thing matters: The prince comes. And he and his princess gallop off into the sunset to live happily ever after.

You might be thinking, *But I'm in real life. And real life is* so *not like fairy tales.*

Or is it? Let me be honest: The evil one wants to keep you and me in prison. But the Prince has come to rescue us so that we may have life (John 10:10).

The apostle Paul says, "He has rescued us from the dominion of darkness and brought us into the kingdom of the Son he loves, in whom we have redemption, the forgiveness of sins" (Colossians 1:13-14).

Jesus has rescued us—not just from a dark castle, but from death and bondage to sin. Sometimes, though, I forget! I forget that I have a real enemy, Satan, who wants to put me in a prison of sin. I forget that I have a real rescuer, Jesus, who has already made a way for me to be saved.

Do you forget sometimes too? Have you forgotten that you're worth saving? Do you feel down and out, as if you're not good enough? As if nobody loves you?

Remember your Rescuer. He took off His royal robes and came down to our level. He took all of God's punishment for our mistakes because we were that important to Him.

Need proof of your worth? Look at the blood of

Jesus. I can't even begin to comprehend what Jesus went through on the cross, but I do know one thing. In God's mind, you were worth dying for.

You *are* important—important enough to be loved and rescued from the sick nastiness of the sin that would have destroyed you. All you have to do is follow Him.

What's a Girl to Do?

If this devotion found you wondering what salvation is, turn back to the very first devotion in this book. Then ask yourself, *Is there any reason why I don't believe this?* If the answer is yes, find some mature believers and keep asking questions as you search for the truth. If the answer is no, trust in Jesus and be rescued from the dominion of darkness.

All in with God

Father, I am amazed by Your love for me. Thank You for this gift of salvation, which comes to me so freely. I don't have to work for it; I just need faith, and faith comes from You. Father, lead me now into a closer walk with You. I long to know You more. In Jesus' name, amen.

A Beauty Like No Other

What matters is not your outer appearance—the styling of your hair, the jewelry you wear, the cut of your clothes—but your inner disposition. Cultivate inner beauty, the gentle, gracious kind that God delights in.
1 PETER 3:3-4 MSG

Cute purses, snazzy earrings, trendy shoes—I love fun, pretty stuff. Maybe you do too. But I'm learning that those things are just accessories to a deeper feminine beauty that God has already placed in my heart.

Stasi Eldredge shares the meaning of being a girl in her book *Captivating*: "God has set within you a femininity that is powerful and tender, fierce and alluring." I love that! In a culture that tells us to make it big—to be popular, famous, thin—and to get guys' attention, it's easy to get so caught up in this real-life beauty pageant that we forget the beauty we already possess. We don't consider the beauty that really matters to God.

God created you uniquely as a girl. And He created you to be beautiful. After all, everything God created,

He called good. But evidently you are more than just good—God is absolutely crazy about you!

How do I know? Because He paid for your sins. He effectively said, "This is how much I love you. This is how beautiful you are. This is how valuable you are to Me." He then stretched out His arms on the cross and died for you! For your mistakes, baggage, and mishaps. For the white lies, big lies, and everything in-between. Even for the stuff nobody knows about.

What does this mean about how we live? I love what Stasi says about a girl who is all in for God: "The gift of our presence is a rare and beautiful gift. To come unguarded, undistracted—and be fully present, fully engaged with whoever we are with at that moment." Jesus, our example, valued the people He talked to. He *really* cared about them. He *really* listened.

And that's what we're called to do too. When we are totally God's, we give the gift of our undivided attention to the people we meet. Not just the stylish girls, the cute guys, or the people we need, but every person. Even those we don't need, and even if they dress differently than we do or talk weird. Christ died for each one.

How often do we judge people based on our first impression? In today's focus verses, Peter says that hairstyles, jewelry, and fashion aren't what really count. Sure, we all love a cute outfit. But Jesus wants us to spend time cultivating inner beauty—the kind that shows up in the way we treat other people. The way we love. The way we act unselfishly. The way we care.

Peter is *not* saying we should walk around with ratty hair and dingy, smelly clothes. A girl who is all in for God takes care of her body because she is a princess of Jesus Christ. But our beauty doesn't depend on how we look. We can be dressed to a *T* but forget the most important part—our hearts.

A girl who is totally God's has a gentle and quiet spirit—a heart that revels in God's love, a heart that loves God first, and a heart that is bubbling over with God's love for every single person.

The next time you pick out an outfit, think about your attitude too. A cute outfit and an ugly, selfish heart just don't match.

What's a Girl to Do?

A gentle and quiet spirit is precious in the sight of God. With that knowledge, pray and ask the Lord to help you become a young woman who desires inner beauty.

All in with God

Father, teach me through Your Word what a gentle and quiet spirit looks like in my life. Renew my mind and transform me so I can realize how precious I am in Your eyes. In Jesus' name, amen.

Temple

Don't you know that you yourselves are God's
temple and that God's Spirit lives in you?
1 CORINTHIANS 3:16

It's my body and I'll do what I want!" The magazine ad I recently read stated exactly what girls believe about their bodies these days. They might say it this way: "It's mine; I can treat it as I want to." Turn on the television, look at a magazine, glance at the Internet, or talk to a friend, and you'll soon come across topics like alcohol and drugs, binging and purging, wearing revealing clothes, and even pornography and casual sex with many partners and both genders.

These all destroy our bodies, which God calls His temple. *Temple?* Yep. It means the place where God lives. In the Old Testament, God's Spirit dwelled in the tabernacle in the wilderness and then the temple in Jerusalem. But when we accept Jesus as our Savior, His Spirit literally moves in—not just for a temporary lease, but forever. God's not renting. He owns you.

What does that mean? That means that you don't own yourself anymore! It's not about knowing *who* you are; it's about knowing *whose* you are. When God sees you, He sees Jesus living in you! That should change the way you see yourself. Paul's message is simple: You belong to God. Period.

You might be thinking, *So what does that mean? I mean, I'm not going to go around wearing a robe and sandals and be a monk.* And I totally agree with you. (I like my heels too much!) But God is telling us we need to look at our bodies differently now that we belong to Him.

You may struggle with some sort of "temple destruction." Maybe you wrestle with an eating disorder or have had sex or are cutting. Or maybe you can't stop getting high or living off of junky foods. Whatever it is, if you are a believer in Jesus Christ, He will help you change the way you live so you can build a healthy, vibrant temple.

You can start by seeking Him, repenting of your ways, and changing your habits. Here's what the Bible says:

> Trust GOD from the bottom of your heart;
> don't try to figure out everything on your own.
> Listen for GOD's voice in everything you do,
> everywhere you go;
> he's the one who will keep you on track.
> Don't assume that you know it all.

Run to GOD! Run from evil!
Your body will glow with health,
your very bones will vibrate with life!
(Proverbs 3:5-8 MSG).

Building healthy temples will make our bodies glow
and our bones vibrate with life! And it will change the
way we live. Before we run off and do something we
might later regret, we need to pray and ask God if what
we're about to do (or not do) is healthy for us. That
might mean saying no to what your friends are doing.
It may mean getting more sleep or waking up earlier
to go exercise.

Whatever the case, make a list of things you need to
change to take care of God's temple—your body. Take
steps today toward new habits and a vibrant, healthy
life in the days ahead.

What's a Girl to Do?

I will repeat the challenge I made above. Ask God
His opinion when you are not absolutely sure if you
should do something. Even when you think you know
the answer, ask Him anyway. Then do what He says.
He will be so pleased you consulted Him and then followed through.

All in with God

Father, this world sends me confusing signals about what is right and wrong. Help me to rely on Your guidance for daily decisions that may have spiritual consequences. I am excited to grow in this area of my relationship with You. In Jesus' name, amen.

Treasure

For where your treasure is, there your heart will be also.
MATTHEW 6:21

When I think of treasure, I think of pirates: buried chests of gold, deserted islands, and Johnny Depp as Captain Jack Sparrow.

But in today's verse, Jesus is talking about something much more valuable than gold. He's talking about how to take care of our hearts.

I *love* going to the mall. Just ask my mom or my best friend! But in this passage, Jesus challenges us to not waste our time storing up or placing too much value on things here on earth. Remember that cute shirt you *had* to have last spring? Do you still have it? Maybe you do, or maybe you don't. It may be a little bit threadbare or even stained. Stuff is just stuff, and it will probably get lost, worn out, or thrown away. It might even somehow disappear into a roommate's closet!

Depressing? No, because Jesus wants us to focus on packing treasure for heaven. God knows how we girls are. The way that we spend our money and our time reveals and even helps determine the desires of our hearts (Matthew 6:19-21). My mom always told me, "If you want to figure out who a girl really is, look at the way she spends her money!"

It's true. Money is a big deal. In fact, Jesus said, "You cannot serve both God and money" (Matthew 6:24). Ouch.

Jesus encouraged His followers (including us girls) to sell their possessions and give to the poor. That doesn't mean Jesus was saying we should never have any money or nice possessions. Rather, He was driving at the *love* of "stuff." It can wield unbelievable power in our minds. And it's easy for a girl to think that money, clothes, or boyfriends will keep us happy. But they won't.

So what's a girl to do?

We need to stop focusing on ourselves. I have come to believe that we build treasures in heaven by giving, not by getting. Taking the time to care about other people— the hurting people in our lives—is the "gold" we can store in heaven. It yields the treasure that lasts forever.

Why is it so hard to live this way? One word: *Satan*.

We are in a battle against evil spirits, not flesh and blood (Ephesians 6:12). And do you know what Satan wants from us more than anything? The evil one wants us to take our eyes off God. He wants us to break ties with the lover of our souls. How does he most often do it?

You got it—through "stuff."

Are the possessions and money in your life distracting your heart? If you really want to know, look at what's most valuable to you. Is it money or clothes? Cell phones or iPods or other people?

Start packing your bags for heaven. Choose to give, not just to get. That's where today's blessings and eternal treasure lie. And no pirate can touch that—not even Captain Jack Sparrow.

What's a Girl to Do?

Putting Jesus and His will first in our lives can be a real challenge. But I pray we are beginning to understand just how important it is not to become captive to the lies of this world. Let's ask God to reveal areas where we have stored treasures here on earth and not in heaven and see if we can change that.

All in with God

Father, I don't want to be caught as a captive in Satan's lies. Help me to use all I have been given—including my money, skills, and possessions—to do as You tell me. I pray that anything I do will glorify You, Lord, and not myself. All glory to You, God, my Father, my King. In Jesus' name, amen.

Living Free

*If God is for us, who can be against
us?...In all these things we are more than
conquerors through him who loved us.*

ROMANS 8:31,37

I heard the song "Nobody Knows It but Me" the other
day, and the words have stuck with me. They describe
someone who says he's dying inside, but nobody else
knows. Sometimes I feel that way—I can wind up feeling pathetic and ashamed, convinced I'm a loser. And
nobody knows it but me. Is that how you would describe
yourself? Every girl struggles with something. And a
lot of times, we don't talk to anybody about it—not
even our best friends.

Is that you? Do you walk around hurting every day,
but nobody has a clue? You can hide behind the makeup
and clothes, but God knows what's in your heart. And He
hurts for you. I believe God weeps over the way our sin
or other people's sin twists the lives of His beloved girls.

Maybe your struggle is one we've already talked about. Or maybe it's so taboo that no one ever talks about it, like pornography, cutting, huffing, or even suicidal thoughts. Maybe you were abused by someone you should have been able to trust. Maybe you've been raped, and you haven't told a soul.

As your sister in Christ, I want you to know one thing: God wants you to be free. *But Megan,* you might be thinking, *there's no hope for me. My life is too screwed up.*

God is bigger than your pain. Consider a girl who was sexually abused by her own dad. She grew up hating him for it. Even worse, she hated herself for letting him do it.

For Lori, life was miserable. The only ways she could make herself feel better were to act out sexually or to get high. And so she did, every day. Most girls who grew up in a situation like this will do anything to feel better. According to the stats, Lori *should* have grown up to be promiscuous and to hate men.

Thankfully, God loves broken people. Jesus said, "It is not the healthy who need a doctor, but the sick" (Mark 2:17). This world is far from perfect. And for those who have been sexually abused, or whose parents have divorced, or who have been bullied at school, or who have lost a close friend, life can be particularly dark.

But Jesus came to heal broken hearts. To free people (like you and me) from the chains of sin and injustice

(Isaiah 61:1). To proclaim, in effect, "My daughter, you are free." Regardless of what you have done or what has been done to you, you don't have to live in guilt and shame. Jesus took your guilt and shame all the way to the grave and buried it there.

The beautiful truth about God is that when we are most broken, He is closest (Psalm 38:17-22). And He's the only one who can make sense of the mess of our lives.

His love is bigger than any hurt. Jesus didn't just put a Band-Aid on our broken heart…He gives us a new heart. He gives us hope. Learn to let His love in. You don't need all that other stuff to feel okay. This is part of being all in for God.

How about you? What's your story? Satan keeps us in bondage to the hurt in our past by keeping us quiet. Do you want to be free? Find someone you trust, someone you look up to, like your mom, a teacher, or a Christian counselor. Tell that person what's going on. Break the silence and be free.

What's a Girl to Do?

If you are hurting because of abuse, addictions, or loss, don't try to make it alone. Get help now. This is not something to take lightly. I love you, and God does even more than me. Take care of yourself.

All in with God

Father, I know I need help. I know others who need help too. Guide me in wisdom to defeat the enemy at his best work—making me believe I am worthless. I am made in Your image, and You love me. May those truths stick like glue to my heart. In Jesus' name, amen.

Faith like a Child's

*Now faith is being sure of what we hope
for and certain of what we do not see.*

HEBREWS 11:1

This verse reminds me of when I was five years old and wanted to go off the diving board *so* bad. But it scared me. The water was so deep, I couldn't touch the bottom. My dad would swim to the end of the diving board, hold his hands up high, and say, "Come on, Megan. You can do it! Trust me." I'd hesitate only a few seconds, and then I'd close my eyes, jump, and scream in joy! Splashing into the water, I'd get wet, but I wouldn't drown because my dad was there to catch me. I had faith in my dad. I had hope that he would catch me. I could see him waiting for me.

But what if your dad isn't around? Or what happens when my dad can't be there for me and I have a difficult decision to make? What do I do when I am figuratively standing on the diving board, wondering if I'll sink or swim, and can't see anybody there to catch me?

Most of us tend to make decisions based on our

own strength. It's like having floaties on our arms. Our decisions are guided by what we know we can accomplish and where we know we'll stay safe. And we put our faith in those things: our intelligence, good looks, athletic ability, musical talent, a likable personality, or...

But faith in God is more than that. It's standing on the end of the diving board without floaties and without anyone there to catch you, yet you know that when you jump, you'll be okay.

The Bible invites us to have faith like a child (Matthew 18:2-4). Run to the diving board with no holds barred. Step out in faith to make a decision, knowing God has your back, that He is good, and that He will always be looking out for your best interest even when you are hurting.

To be totally God's, we must have faith. Without it, we can't possibly please God, because anyone who comes to Him must believe that He exists and that He rewards those who seek Him (Hebrews 11:3,6). God is the only one who can fill the hole in our soul, comfort our loneliness, soothe our hurt and pain, forgive us for our mistakes, and guide our decisions.

Consider today what you are placing your faith in more than God. Is anything holding you back from running into His arms and trusting Him with reckless abandon, just as a child would? Write those things on a piece of paper and begin praying over them today, asking God to strengthen your faith in areas where you lack it. He will be pleased that you are faithful enough already to ask Him to strengthen your faith.

What's a Girl to Do?

Faith is a term we have grown up with in the church, but I believe we have forgotten its true importance. A solid relationship with Christ is based on faith alone. Begin to trust in Jesus today.

All in with God

Father, I love You! With all my being I want this to be true. I don't want to live as if I don't believe, because I do. Help my unbelief, Lord. Grow my faith in You! In Jesus' name, amen.

Stardust in His Hands

The LORD knows the thoughts of man,
that they are a mere breath.

PSALM 94:11 NASB

Do you believe God can heal someone? That He can really reach down and touch a grandparent who has cancer, an aunt who was critically injured in a car accident, or a friend who's hurting so bad, she's cutting?

Or think about this. Do you believe God is there for us in the middle of a family crisis, the loss of a loved one, or a breakup? Is He there when a tornado rips through your neighborhood, tearing apart homes and businesses for miles around?

In the Bible, Job had to face some of these difficult questions about God.

Job desired to please God, to listen to Him and obey Him. The Bible says Job turned away from sin (Job 1:8). Completely blameless and always pure, Job was a man of integrity. But Satan didn't think Job's commitment to God was real. He thought Job was fake. So he challenged God to allow him to test Job and make Job's life straight-up miserable. God agreed to the test, so Satan destroyed Job's life. Here's what he took away from him:

- Job's animals were stolen. A lot of them—7000 sheep, 3000 camels, 500 yoke of oxen, and 500 donkeys. These weren't just animals; they were Job's income.

- All of his workers were killed.

- His seven sons and three daughters were crushed when their house collapsed.

- Job himself got really sick. Big, nasty sores covered his whole body.

And that was in just one day!

But even though Job's life fell apart, he didn't. His wife did though. She told him to curse God and die (Job 2:9). (Marriage 101: As a wife, don't ever advise your husband to do this.) Job didn't listen. In fact, Job did not sin even once. He was confused though. Hurting deeply, he asked God something like this: "What on earth are You doing?" But listen to how God responds:

> Where were you when I laid the earth's
> foundation?
> Tell me, if you understand.

Who marked off its dimensions? Surely
you know!
Who stretched a measuring line across it?
On what were its footings set,
or who laid its cornerstone—
while the morning stars sang together
and all the angels shouted for joy?
(Job 38:4-7).

Right then, at that moment, Job got it. He remained
sinless and proved Satan wrong.

This same God holds the entire world in the palm
of His hand. He counts all of the stars and names them
too. We are made from dust; He holds stardust in His
hands. We think we're smart; He *made* smart. We use
words to communicate; He uses words to create.

The best part is that this same God, who ended up
blessing Job with twice as much as he had before, is also
a very personal God. He loves the world, but He also
loves *you*. Though your thoughts are but a mere breath
to the Lord of the universe, He notices the tiniest breath
you take. Today, breathe deeply and know that as God
holds the world in His hands, He is thinking about you.

What's a Girl to Do?

When life is difficult and you're having a hard time
understanding what's going on around you, step back

for a moment, take a deep breath, and remind yourself
how big God really is. Read Psalms. And pray that God
will reveal His character to you in the midst of the storm.

All in with God

Father, forgive me when I forget to worship You as I
should. Remind me who You are, Lord, and help me to think
about Your love, might, and wonder. Bring me back to the
true reality: I worship the one true God. Deepen my rela-
tionship with You through Jesus Christ. In His name, amen.

Bloom Where You Are Planted

*Who knows? Maybe you were made
queen for just such a time as this.*
ESTHER 4:13 MSG

When I was little, my dad read to me every night. One story I remember in particular is *Beauty and the Beast*. I joined in the story and became a character. It never got old.

As I've gotten older, I find myself loving to read exciting stories, like mystery novels or romantic comedies with cute guys. Fascination takes hold of my heart as I dive into stories with twists, turns, and happy endings.

I am amazed at the many wonderful and adventurous stories in the Bible. Stories about the world around us and how it was created. Stories of family and friendship. Battles won and lost, love and romance, and so much more! One of my favorite Bible stories is the story of Esther, a young girl who became queen. Listen to the story:

King Ahasuerus was looking for a new queen. He

got rid of the former queen because she did not do what he wanted her to do. Wow! So his advisors suggested he bring in all the young maidens of Persia, hold a beauty pageant, and pick one. Imagine that!

He chose Esther. The story goes on to say that even though Esther did not want to be queen, she agreed. Esther was an orphan being raised by her cousin, Mordecai, whom she trusted with all her heart. Mordecai was faithful to God and encouraged Esther to stand strong by saying the words in today's focus verse. And you know what? Esther, because she was the queen, was able to save all of her people (the Jews), including herself, from being killed! What strength, courage, and faith she displayed!

Take time today to read the book of Esther. It's short, so you can do it all at once. You will be blessed and encouraged! I am every time I read it. God's fingerprints are clearly evident even though His name is not mentioned in the book. I am always reminded how much He is in control of my life—regardless of the circumstance.

I love the saying "Bloom where you are planted!" Wherever you are in your own life story, remember that God is in control. He wants to use you right where you are. Open your eyes today and see where He wants you to serve. See where He wants you to go. Trust and follow Him, and be ready for the adventure of a lifetime!

What's a Girl to Do?

Think about the people around you, where you often go, and what you do in your daily routine. Pull out your journal or a piece of paper and begin to think of ways you can show the love of Christ to your circle of influence—your Persia—and start blooming today!

All in with God

Father, open my eyes to the world around me—my circle of influence, where You have placed me. Help me see Your purpose for placing me here! May I be used for Your glory always. In Jesus' name, amen.

Me, Me, Me

You ask and do not receive, because you ask with wrong motives, so that you may spend it on your pleasures.

JAMES 4:3 NASB

Have you ever wondered whether God really hears you when you pray? Or do you pray about something that never seems to get answered—at least not the way you wanted it to? This has happened to me quite often. At times like that, I feel as though God may not even be listening to me. Have you been there?

On the other hand, on some days my relationship with God seems so close. I pray and talk with Him and can see Him working in my life and answering my prayers.

When Jesus prayed in Gethsemane, just prior to being taken captive to be crucified on the cross, He prayed a prayer I think we all would have prayed. He basically said something like this: *Father, if at all possible, please take this cup from Me. I don't want to have to go through this. Is there another way?* I think if we were in Jesus' shoes, we would have stopped our prayer right there. *God, help me get out of this!* Thankfully, Jesus continued: *If there's no other way, I certainly understand. I want to do Your will.*

Jesus had it figured out. He knew that the reason He was on this earth was to live out the Father's will for His life. Therefore, instead of just praying for what He wanted (which He did), He threw another possibility out there: *Yet I will do whatever You want Me to, Father. I am here for You.* Jesus didn't push His own agenda. He did not ask with wrong motives. He prayed not that His will be done, but that His Father's will be done.

Rarely do I hear Christians pray for God's will regardless of the outcome. Why don't we pray like this? I think it's because we're scared to ask for God's will. We fear the outcome. We fear being left to deal with heartache. Or we struggle to believe He has our best interests at heart.

When we get to know other people really well, we see who they are beneath the surface. We see how much they care and love us, and trusting them becomes easier. Even if what is ahead may be scary and undesirable, tackling the problem is easier when we can lean on a relationship built on trust.

Relationships are built on good communication. If we desire to be all in for God, we need to work on communicating with Him—not just telling Him our desires, but also listening for His desires for us. God knows that His will for my life is so much better than my own. When I approach Him in prayer, I have to be convinced that He knows me better than I know myself. Jesus knew this. And He was tremendously close with the Father as a result. I believe their close relationship made it much easier for Jesus to say and truly mean, "I want Your will, Father, not Mine."

Spend time with your heavenly Father today. Ask Him how to trust Him with His will for your life. Then be open to His leading and what He may be showing you!

What's a Girl to Do?

Let's attempt to test ourselves for "selfish" prayers. Listen as you pray. Listen to your heart and ask the Spirit to guide you to pray with right motives—with God's will in mind, not yours.

All in with God

Father, You are awesome, and I desire to know You and Your will for my life better. Daily I make selfish decisions and even pray selfish prayers. Move me to pray in a more humble way. I love You! In Jesus' name, amen.

Overcomer

I have told you these things, so that in me you may
have peace. In this world you will have trouble.
But take heart! I have overcome the world.

JOHN 16:33

I love watching my little brother play sports. He is
really good. And he has also been very fortunate to
play on a lot of winning teams. His baseball team fin-
ished fifth in the nation when he was just 11 years old.

I, on the other hand, have not been as fortunate.
I have been on some losing teams through the years.
The difference, though (and don't tell Zach I said this),
is that he takes losing a little harder than I did.

Losing in sports is one thing. Losing in life is quite
another. Maybe you didn't pass a test even though you
studied like crazy for it. Or you applied for a job but
didn't get it, or a relationship didn't work out, or you
didn't make a spot on a team or a choir. Life can be
hard on us, but we don't need to be hard on ourselves.
I have come to learn the difference between losing and
being a loser.

On several occasions, Jesus warned His disciples about His impending death on the cross. (Talk about hard times!) In today's focus verse, we see Him adding something like this: "I've told you this now so you won't fear, but rather will have peace. In the world you'll have trouble—no question about it. But you're in Me, and remember, I've overcome the world."

I looked up the word *overcome* to see what Jesus was referring to. It means to prevail, conquer, or defeat. When we're going through a difficult time and feel as if we're losing in the game of life, how can we keep the attitude of a conqueror? It comes by faith (1 John 5:4). Our unshakable belief in Jesus gives us the spirit of a war hero so we can prevail and conquer in His name.

What we conquer, though, is not physical things, but things like sin, hopelessness, sadness, brokenness, defeat...all of the emotions that tear us apart. We conquer lies, like the belief that our mistakes make us losers. You and I *will* mess up sometimes. After all, we're human. Satan sneers when we degrade ourselves, and he enjoys seeing people hurt us. The devil loves it when we believe that we are losers, that we're stuck, that we're not good enough.

I know life's not fair. It never will be. But this does not change the most powerful truth: We are already on the side of the true winner. Through Christ, we can prevail over the label *loser*.

Jesus *has* overcome the world. When He chose to come to earth and live as a man (Philippians 2:7-8), never sin (2 Corinthians 5:21), and then die on the cross and rise again so all who believe will live (Colossians 1:20,22), He won. And He didn't just win a gold medal and take a victory lap. He defeated death. And when we are in Him, we win too.

Truth is powerful. The Bible says that in Christ, we can overcome, prevail, and conquer sin, temptation, doubt, addiction, abuse...whatever.

Don't give up on yourself. God hasn't given up on you! And a relationship with Him changes everything!

What's a Girl to Do?

Don't give up. Don't listen to the lies of the world. We are not losers, but winners. The world may not acknowledge that, but that's because the world doesn't want to acknowledge Christ. Be strong and live by faith.

All in with God

Father, I am so thankful that I am in You. You are the winner. I have overcome because I am in You. Thank You for this promise. Help me to live out this truth. In Jesus' name, amen.

On the Front Line

Put on the full armor of God, so that you will be able
to stand firm against the schemes of the devil.

EPHESIANS 6:11 NASB

I love to think about the wonderful summer nights I've enjoyed looking at the stars. The moon shines down; friends and family join together to sing, laugh, and tell funny stories around a campfire; and don't forget the s'mores! Ah, the joys of summer.

Sitting peacefully next to the fire, you feel a sudden sting. Then another. You smack your leg. Then your arm. The next thing you know, mosquitoes are everywhere. It's a covert attack! Before long you find yourself dancing around to the music of the mosquitoes, smacking yourself like a loon. I hate bugs!

Mosquitoes are one thing. The spiritual attack we're under is quite another. When I first learned about our spiritual battle, I was scared and excited at the same time. I thought, *Yeah, I'm tough—let's go!* But then I changed my mind. *Wait! I didn't sign up to be a soldier. I'm not in the army. I don't want to fight!* But the truth is, a battle is raging. It's invisible, but it's real.

> Be prepared. You're up against far more than you can handle on your own. Take all the help you can get, every weapon God has issued, so that when it's all over but the shouting you'll still be on your feet. Truth, righteousness, peace, faith, and salvation are more than words. Learn to apply them. You'll need them throughout your life. God's Word is an indispensable weapon. In the same way, prayer is essential in this ongoing warfare. Pray hard and long. Pray for your brothers and sisters. Keep your eyes open. Keep each other's spirits up so that no one falls behind or drops out (Ephesians 6:13-18 MSG).

When the apostle Paul wrote those words, he lived in an age that was different from ours. In the twenty-first century, warfare is primarily electronic, not hand-to-hand. We don't carry swords or worry too much about being close to the battlefront. But maybe we should. The front lines are closer than we think.

Fencing classes might be a blast, but I don't think we should all hurry to sign up. I was thinking we should start more Bible studies and prayer groups. The weapons God wants us to use come from a close relationship with Him and fellowship with other believers.

Did you notice in the Scripture above how important prayer is? It's essential to help us during battle. And did you see the emphasis on the Word of God? It's described as an "indispensable weapon." Both are vital to help us be more aware of our enemy and his attacks.

What if we did start Bible studies and prayer groups? Do you think they would make a difference? I do! The Bible describes the devil as a prowling lion ready to devour us (1 Peter 5:8). But we have the victor on our side—Jesus Christ! He has already defeated Satan, and death has no power over those who believe in Jesus. By preparing for battle (reading the Word and praying) we will have success on the battlefield.

Truth, righteousness, peace, faith, and salvation. All of us have full access to this armor. Start training today!

What's a Girl to Do?

You and I should begin to prepare for battle right now. From the instant we wake up in the morning to our final waking moments before we drift off to sleep at night, we are in a spiritual battle. We must prepare and know God's battle plan (it's found in His Word). Begin today to study, prepare, and ask for God's wisdom to discern the enemy's strategy for attacking you.

All in with God

Father, You have provided me with the tools to stand against my enemy. Thank You! I know Satan can use other people to hurt me, but my true enemy is him—the devil. I love You, Lord. Help me be a prepared soldier in the battle that is already raging around me. In Jesus' name, amen.

Undeserved

*He said to me, "My grace is sufficient for you, for
my power is made perfect in weakness." Therefore I
will boast all the more gladly about my weaknesses,
so that Christ's power may rest on me.*

2 CORINTHIANS 12:9

Have you ever taken an exam and gotten a really bad
grade? (If you're breathing, I'm sure you can say
yes. But if the answer is no, we'll see you at Harvard in
a few years.) As you stare with horror at the bad grade
on your exam, you suddenly hear the teacher or pro-
fessor say, "I'm going to curve the exam by ten points.
Keep working hard."

Party time! You were given a better grade even
though you know you didn't deserve it. That's grace!
Grace is when you are given something you don't deserve.

And God is full of grace. We haven't earned His love,
His protection, or His provision. Yet He still offers these
things freely and willingly. And He does so for anyone
regardless of whether she meets His standard of being
good enough, which is good news because none of us
meet that standard anyway.

We know that humans are sinful. Sometimes we see an undeserving person get a break, and we think, *Of all people, why did she get that? A lot of other people deserve it more than she does.* But really, none of us deserve the good things God gives us.

The apostle Paul understood God's grace better than most people do:

> So I wouldn't get a big head, I was given the gift of a handicap to keep me in constant touch with my limitations. Satan's angel did his best to get me down; what he in fact did was push me to my knees. No danger then of walking around high and mighty! At first I didn't think of it as a gift, and begged God to remove it. Three times I did that, and then God told me, "My grace is enough; it's all you need. My strength comes into its own in your weakness."
>
> Once I heard that, I was glad to let it happen. I quit focusing on the handicap and began appreciating the gift. It was a case of Christ's strength moving in on my weakness. Now I take limitations

> in stride, and with good cheer, these
> limitations that cut me down to size—
> abuse, accidents, opposition, bad breaks.
> I just let Christ take over! And so the
> weaker I get, the stronger I become
> (2 Corinthians 12:9-10 MSG).

When Jesus said that His grace was sufficient for Paul, He was basically saying that life with hard times *and* His grace was better than life with no hard times at all. My first reaction is, *I'd much rather not have the problems, Jesus.* But the more I think about it, the more I see what Jesus meant. If Paul had no hard times, he would have never understood God's grace the way he did. When I am at my lowest or think I have nothing to offer, that's when God's power is most obvious.

The Bible says we're not to be ashamed of the gospel, for it is the power of God for our salvation (Romans 1:16). We receive this salvation not by works, but by grace (2 Timothy 1:8-10 NASB). So what do we know of grace so far?

- Grace does not involve work.
- It is undeserved—like receiving something for nothing.
- God shows us grace with His love.

Whenever I think about God's grace, I can't help but remember these lines from one of the most popular hymns of all time:

> *Amazing grace, how sweet the sound*
> *That saved a wretch like me.*
> *I once was lost, but now I'm found,*
> *Was blind but now I see!*

Grace is love that came down from heaven before we ever asked. We didn't deserve it. I love that about God. He gives it anyway because He loves you and me! Make a list of the ways God has given you His grace, and thank Him today for these amazing gifts!

What's a Girl to Do?

Without grace, we'd be on a never-ending trail of tears and heartache. God has given us His love and salvation as gifts. Even with Christ evident in the world, we still see people around us suffering such pain. Let's show grace to others today by sharing the gifts He's given us!

All in with God

Father, I desire to know You more—Your purposes, Your love, and Your grace. I am beginning to see that I should be grateful for all that I have. So thank You, Lord. I love You! In Jesus' name, amen.

Control Freak

In his heart a man plans his course, but
the LORD determines his steps.

PROVERBS 16:9

I hate change. I hate letting go most of all. I remember
when my boyfriend was leaving town for my senior
year. I was faced with this fact about myself—I'm not
very good at good-byes. I guess I get pretty attached to
anyone or anything that is important to me.

My mom recalls a story from my childhood. I had
a puppy named Rio, and my dad would occasionally let
him loose. Rio would run away as fast as he could, and I
would run after him, crying and screaming until my dad,
after a fierce chase, would place him back into my arms.

Are you like me? Do you fear or hate change? I want
to share one of my journal entries about being lonely.

> Why is being alone so...lonely? I need to
> know my boyfriend loves me, and yet I do
> know it. How is that logical? How does

that make sense? I feel like we are beginning this college separation. And just so
you know—it's hard!

When I realized how lonely I was after he left for
college, I knew I had to turn back to God and give Him
His rightful place in my heart. My desperation after a
boy left showed the major place he had in my life—the
place of priority that God should have and no one or
nothing else.

I bet my need to feel in control has something to
do with all of this. I don't like the idea of things being
completely out of my hands. Can you relate? Thinking
about someone else doing everything for me drives me
crazy. Brushing our hair, helping us write our names,
tying our shoes...as infants and toddlers we needed
others to help us with small tasks. When I grew out
of that stage, I thought I didn't need any more help.
Even from God.

Now that you're older, what things can make you
feel out of control? How about questions like these:

- Will the popular crowd like you?
- Will a boy think you're cute?
- Will you make the cut on the team?
- Will that zit on your forehead disappear?
- Will your friend move away?

You know, we girls like to have things our way. We want what we want, when we want it. And we usually want it *now*! Some of us are pretty used to getting our way. We can have some influence on some of the things I listed above, but mostly we have little say about them.

Change happens. The best way to deal with change is to come to the same conclusion I did when my boyfriend left. I realized I needed to turn back to God and give Him His rightful place in my heart.

Regardless of whether you struggle with change, Christ deserves to reign as King in your heart. Allow Him to sit on the throne of your life, and you will find true joy!

What's a Girl to Do?

Change and letting go of control are two difficult topics to tackle. They are complex and can relate to experiences from our childhoods. I pray that each of us can make progress in giving control over to the Lord.

All in with God

Father, help me to give everything to You. You have shown me a glimpse of how much You love me. I trust in You. Give me the strength to place even the little parts of my life into Your skillful hands. I love You! In Jesus' name, amen.

CHOICES, DECISIONS, CONSEQUENCES

Devotions on the power of choice and deciding to live for Christ

Soul Poison

Forget about deciding what's right for each other.
Here's what you need to be concerned about:
that you don't get in the way of someone else,
making life more difficult than it already is.

ROMANS 14:13 MSG

One of the greatest debates I have heard among Christians is whether or not it is acceptable to drink alcohol, smoke, chew, and date boys who do. Ha ha—I'm slightly kidding, but the truth is, there are a number of things we Christians don't have a lot of answers to.

Still, many Christians today are quick to make judgments about somebody's character and spiritual growth based on behaviors that tend to be questionable—*to them*. In Romans, Paul addresses this dilemma.

> None of us are permitted to insist on our own way in these matters. It's God we are answerable to...not each other... Forget

about deciding what's right for each other. Here's what you need to be concerned
about: that you don't get in the way of
someone else, making life more difficult
than it already is...

If you confuse others by making a big issue
over what they eat or don't eat, you're no
longer a companion with them in love, are
you? These, remember, are persons for
whom Christ died. Would you risk sending them to hell over an item in their diet?
Don't you dare let a piece of God-blessed
food become an occasion of soul-poisoning!
(Romans 14:7-8,13,15-16 MSG).

We must also be careful that our own self-criticism
doesn't cause others to stumble as well. Here's an example: You and Julie are friends. Julie is a new believer,
and she looks to you for answers to questions about
being a Christian. God has given you many opportunities to speak the truth into Julie's life. One day, Julie
confides in you that she is anorexic and struggling with
her weight. You explain to her that her body is God's
home and she is made in His image. You express your
desire to help her through this difficult time.

The next day, you and Julie go to lunch. After you get your food and sit at the table, you say, "I hate my body. I so need to lose some weight before homecoming." And you proceed to shove your tray of food to the side, sipping a soda instead.

See the problem? You told Julie she needs help, but now you keep yourself from eating in front of her, reinforcing the message she already struggles with: *I'm fat. Nobody will like me unless I lose weight.* Can she really listen to your advice or look up to you as a stronger believer now?

I'm not perfect. I struggle with judging myself and other people too. We all do. But I desire with all my heart to do as God says and make life easier for others, not more difficult. I hope you do too. Whether it's seeing somebody behaving a certain way you don't agree with or behaving in a way that will cause somebody else to stumble, be careful of not being quick to "soul poison" anybody. If we can accomplish this, even on small scale, we will be making a real difference in people's lives and be that much closer to being all in for God.

What's a Girl to Do?

Let's try to keep from judging others—not just this week, but for good. Ask God to convict you when you begin to say something you shouldn't.

All in with God

Father, it is so easy to say something mean or judgmental. Everyone does it. Help me to be a good witness to those around me. I desire to open my mouth in love and purity. I love You, Lord. In Jesus' name, amen.

Life Outside the Bubble

We don't have a priest who is out of touch with
our reality. He's been through weakness and
testing, experienced it all—all but the sin. So
let's walk right up to him and get what he is so
ready to give. Take the mercy, accept the help.
HEBREWS 4:15 MSG

Picture this: You and several friends decide to hang at Rob's house. Popcorn and a movie. Everyone hurries to find a decent seat in Rob's living room. You told your parents of the movie night at Rob's, and they did what they always do—they called Rob's parents to find out what the movie was. They thought the film was okay, so you were good to go.

Into the living room walks Rob. "Hey, my parents are asleep. Let's watch a different movie—one with a little more 'action,' if you know what I mean."

Then the movie comes on. "A little more action" doesn't come close to describing this film. You want to close your eyes at all the violence, evil, and nudity, but you are too embarrassed. Now the images are burned in your brain, and you're afraid to walk the two blocks home alone in the dark.

Ugh...what should you do?

Ever felt that way? Leaving Rob's house would have been like committing social suicide, but that probably would have been the best move.

Protecting our eyes and ears is a constant battle. We are bombarded with images of blood, violence, and nudity in the movies and on TV. And unfortunately, vulgar language, sexual harassment, and physical abuse are sad realities in many of our lives. What do we do? We can't walk around with paper bags over our heads and earplugs stuck in our ears. That would be pretty dangerous, and we'd look a bit strange!

It comes down to making better choices. If something will cause us to hear or see something we shouldn't, we can always change course and veer another direction. Jesus tells us that He always leaves a door open for escape when we're in over our heads (1 Corinthians 10:13).

The images or voices you've seen and heard will come back when you least expect them. Before you know it, you will find yourself unaffected and tempted to go along with things you really don't believe in.

This is not the goal. As girls who are all in for God, we need to ask Jesus to help us stay strong in the middle of hard situations. He's been through it all and understands our weaknesses, as our focus verse reminds us.

Sure, it would be easier to live in a bubble and never be around sin. But that's impossible while on earth. Remember, we can do all things through Christ who gives us strength (Philippians 4:13). We can walk out on movies, ask others to tone down the language, and live purely in a sinful world. God promises to give you the strength.

Take care of your eyes. Be bold and faithfully stand firm today and always!

What's a Girl to Do?

Let's make a specific effort to stand out for Christ. Let's pray and ask God to help us be bold and do what's right.

All in with God

Father, this world is full of temptations, full of things that fill my mind with unrighteousness. I know I don't always avoid these situations. Sometimes I can even run toward them. I want to change. Help me to not become like the bad things I see and hear. Guard my mind and spirit and give me the strength to choose to do what is right. I love You, Jesus! In Your name, amen.

So You Think You've Got Talent?

Well done, good and faithful servant! You have been faithful with a few things; I will put you in charge of many things. Come and share your master's happiness!

MATTHEW 25:21

Talented people come in all shapes, sizes, and ages. When they put their talent to work, they are so good at what they do, they beat all the competition and make a name for themselves.

But what about people who have talent but don't care? They come in all shapes and sizes too. They are still good at what they do, but they are either too scared or too lazy to practice and become the best. Many of us have seen their ability and know they would go far—if they only tried.

Jesus told a lot of stories when He walked the earth. One was about talents. A talent in Jesus' day was a unit of weight (one talent was about seventy-five pounds). People measured money by weighing it, so in this case, a talent is a pile of gold or some other precious stone or metal. As Jesus' parable became famous, people began to refer to special abilities as talents.

The parable of the talents is about a man who entrusts some of his property to his servants. One servant received five talents, another received two talents, and another received one. The servant with five talents immediately invested his five talents and gained five more. The servant with two talents did the same and gained two more talents. But the servant with one talent dug a hole in the ground and buried his master's money.

When the master returned, he said something like this: "Okay, so what did you do with what I gave you?" The master was pleased with the investment and return of the first two servants. But the servant who buried his talent did not get such a happy response. The master was so upset with his final servant that he took the talent back.

Which servant reminds you most of yourself? Are you like the first servant, who has lots of talent and uses it wisely for God? Are you like the second servant, who has a little talent but uses it for God? Or are you like the third servant, who didn't invest his talent for God at all?

If the third servant had done as his master requested, he probably would have received the same happy response. He would have been told, "Well done; I am pleased with you."

Here's the bottom line: Whatever your "talent" situation may be, don't be like the third servant and bury your gifts until our Master's return. Instead, use what God has entrusted to you for His glory. One of the best gifts He has given us is the gift of eternal life through His Son Jesus (Romans 6:23). Begin with that. You have the gift of salvation! Share it. Tell others. What else has He given you? Invest your gift, and God will bring the increase!

What's a Girl to Do?

Pray and ask the Lord what gifts you have and how you can use them for Him. Then wait on Him—He'll let you know. Remember, no one but God may notice what you do. Don't worry about whether others see. God is the only one who matters!

All in with God

Father, You are a wonderful Master who gives good gifts. I want to use the talents You have entrusted to me exactly the way You have intended. Please guide me. I really want to do Your will with what You have given me. I love You! In Jesus' name, amen.

Claim the Victory

*I do not understand what I do. For what I want
to do I do not do, but what I hate I do.*

ROMANS 7:15

Remember watching old cartoons and seeing a character who had a moral dilemma? An angel and a demon appear on his shoulders. As the cartoon character thinks about what decision to make, the demon whispers his tempting enticements: "Go ahead, no one will notice...C'mon, this will be fun...Don't be such a chicken..."

The angel defends what is good and says, "Careful, you may regret this later...Someone will get hurt...Don't follow the crowd...Do the right thing..."

Sounds kind of like real life, huh? These voices represent our conscience. But I think the spiritual battle raging around us is bigger than we realize. I believe those old cartoons were closer to the truth than we know.

When we face a moral dilemma, we often have thoughts about what may feel good, what may seem fun, what consequences may occur, and the risks of getting caught. We all have weak areas bent toward sin, and the enemy knows this.

The apostle Paul was acutely aware of his weakness. In today's verses, Paul explains how he continually struggles with the pull of sin in his life. Sin can lead even some of the strongest Christians to make poor decisions. Yet Paul had hope.

> If I know the law but still can't keep it, and if the power of sin within me keeps sabotaging my best intentions, I need help! I realize I don't have what it takes. I decide to do good, but I don't really do it...I truly delight in God's commands, but it's pretty obvious that not all of me joins in that delight...The answer, thank God, is that Jesus Christ can and does (Romans 7:20-25 MSG).

Wow! Paul basically says that we are helpless to defeat sin without Christ. We're in an invisible spiritual battle. If we are in Christ, we have the Spirit of God and have been released or freed from the power of sin. God offered His own sinless life as a sacrifice for you and me. He defeated the sin that entangles us every day. Praise the Lord!

Lean on the power of the Holy Spirit. Listen to His still, small voice telling you the right way to go. Ask for God's wisdom and claim the victory over sin in your life today!

What's a Girl to Do?

We all make mistakes. We fall into sin, and Satan pushes us down, hoping we will forget that we have freedom through Christ. We need to set our minds on the things of the Spirit. If you're not sure what those are, read the Bible. Romans 8:5 is a good place to start.

All in with God

Father, I do not want to sin. I know that I'm young in my faith and that as I choose to grow in You, Your Spirit will help me to become strong. I long for that, Lord. Help me to begin to follow the leading of Your Spirit so I can win the battle over sin. In Jesus' name, amen.

Fix Your Eyes

I denied myself nothing my eyes desired; I refused my heart no pleasure. My heart took delight in all my work, and this was the reward for all my labor. Yet when I surveyed all that my hands had done and what I had toiled to achieve, everything was meaningless, a chasing after the wind; nothing was gained under the sun.

ECCLESIASTES 2:10-11

recently heard an incredible definition for the word *tragedy*: "succeeding in the things of life that don't matter." It made me think about the things I spend time on, get obsessed with, and cry over that really don't matter.

Our culture seems to be obsessed with success. It defines success by the amount of money we have, how well we're known, or how many friends we have. We may be successful if we've achieved recognition for something we did, like receiving an award at school, winning a sports championship, or being elected class president. Such achievements are wonderful and should be noted.

But at the end of the day, I'm telling you now, the trophies will collect dust. Lots of dust!

I struggle with this as much as anyone. Many times, I don't give God the glory He deserves. I totally forget or neglect to acknowledge who really did the work. Here's what should go through my head: First, God made me. I wouldn't be here without Him. Second, He gives me the talents I have and opportunities to use them. Third, successes that come from those opportunities are all gifts from Him (James 1:17).

I'm not taking anything away from your own efforts. You have to work hard to accomplish great things. God calls us to work hard, to run the race, to strive for the best. But it should all be for His glory! Don't strive to measure up to the world's standards. Paul wrote that we should "fix our eyes not on what is seen but on what is unseen, for what is seen is temporary and what is unseen is eternal" (2 Corinthians 4:18). The things in this life are fleeting. She who dies with the most toys, still dies. Are you fixing your eyes on the unseen? Or are you chasing after success as the world defines it?

Ask God today to show you what true success is. Remember, success should reveal eternal significance. Live with that goal in mind. And remember to give Him the glory!

What's a Girl to Do?

Are you succeeding in life at things that don't matter?

All in with God

Father, I love to call You Father. You are my true Daddy—Abba. I love You. Please help me to not be afraid to look different from people who are enamored with this world. Give me the heart to follow You, Lord, regardless of where You may lead me. Show me the true meaning of success and to focus on that. In Jesus' name, amen.

Searching God's Heart

We are destroying speculations and every lofty thing
raised up against the knowledge of God, and we are
taking every thought captive to the obedience of Christ.

2 CORINTHIANS 10:5 NASB

I love the book *Confessions of a Shopaholic*! And when the movie came out recently, my mom and I were among the first in line at our local theater to see it. We had a great time laughing until we hurt and elbowing each other when we could relate to what was happening on-screen. My belly and side ached for days!

The movie depicts a life lived on impulse. Becky Bloomwood is the main character, who struggles to control her desire to shop. Becky views shopping as a stress reliever and gives in to her internal impulses to buy whatever she believes she needs—until she receives her credit card bill. Wow! Once she is faced with reality and enormous debt, she begins to understand the importance of thinking before acting!

Oswald Chambers, who wrote the devotional *My Utmost for His Highest,* said this about 2 Corinthians

10:5: "So much Christian work today has never been disciplined, but has simply come into being by impulse… But true determination and zeal are found in obeying God, not in the inclination to serve Him that arises from our own undisciplined human nature."

Mr. Chambers is criticizing the "do it now" mentality. He says we need to take our thoughts captive, make them prisoners for Jesus, and do what He wants for our lives.

Have you ever noticed that many mature Christians take time and think before they act? They pray and search God's heart on issues before making decisions. Mr. Chambers tells us that these Christians are disciplining their thoughts and actions. They don't quickly do what they want, but consider first what God wants and choose to do His will.

God says not to be impulsive. If the apostle James used today's vernacular, he might have said, "Listen. Don't be thinking you know the future—'cuz you don't. Only God does. And it's His will that will be done. So you better talk to Him before you announce any plans." (See James 4:12-15.)

God desires that you rely on His will. Align your life, thoughts, dreams, desires, and passions with His. When you do, you won't be disappointed! And you may even be able to keep your green scarf. (You've just got to read the book!)

What's a Girl to Do?

I'm convicted that our world is all about instant gratification. Do it now or else. God wants us to wait on Him and His will (Psalm 27:14). No more jumping the gun. Instead, let's ask for God's help today in waiting on His will in our lives.

All in with God

Father, sometimes out of good intentions I do things quickly and then regret my rash decisions. But You even use that to teach me a valuable lesson: I need to wait on You and seek Your will, not mine. Show me Your will, Lord, today and always. In Jesus' name, amen.

Bananas, Strawberries, and Self-Control

The fruit of the Spirit is love, joy, peace, patience, kindness, goodness, faithfulness, gentleness, and self-control. Against such things there is no law.

GALATIANS 5:22-23

Do you like the title of today's devotional? When I hear the word *fruit*, I instantly picture ripe red strawberries, curvy yellow bananas, juicy green apples, and fuzzy peaches. The last thing that comes to my mind is the fruit of the Spirit. But the fruit of the Spirit is the behavioral goal list for Christians.

I'm lucky if I show a few of these character traits, let alone all of them! Seeing this fruit grow in our lives seems too much to hope for. How can we do it? The Bible tells us that by living by God's Spirit, we won't be so tempted to sin (Galatians 5:16). When we're led by the Spirit, we'll naturally do good things in the name of Christ. If we are living by the Spirit, we may reach out to a hurting classmate or even someone we don't know very well. But we do it all through the love of Jesus working through us—not in our own strength.

Reading the Old Testament, you'll get an idea of all the rules the Israelites had to follow. But did you know that God gave them the Law so they would realize they *can't* do it alone? So their own sin would get in the way of ever being able to obey the Law? God wanted them and us to see that following the Law or being saved and producing fruit are impossible because of our sin. We can't do it! We always mess up. This helps us understand how awesome Jesus' sacrifice really was!

The fruit of the Spirit has to grow in us. This growth occurs through an ongoing, close relationship with God through Jesus. The more we deny doing only what we want to do, the more we will begin to notice the sprouting of this wonderful fruit in our lives.

What's a Girl to Do?

We can do nothing apart from God. He is the one who gives us faith to believe and be saved, and He is the one who helps us turn away from our sinful nature. So the best way to begin growing fruit is to pray through each item in Galatians 5:22-23 and ask God to grow each one in you. Then watch for opportunities and listen for His guidance in your life.

All in with God

Father, thank You for the gift of the Holy Spirit, who guides me in love to bear fruit that lasts. Enable me through Your Spirit to deny my desire to sin and to live Your way. I love You, Lord. In Jesus' name, amen.

The Greatest Love

If we confess our sins, He is faithful and
righteous to forgive us our sins and to
cleanse us from all unrighteousness.
1 JOHN 1:9 NASB

When I was a little girl, I woke up one morning and decided that for one day, I would be perfect. I wouldn't get sassy with my mom. I wouldn't get annoyed by my little brother's whining. Somehow, I thought that if I just tried hard enough, I could be good.

But let's face it—we all mess up sometimes. Maybe we pass notes in class, cheat on a test, or spread rumors about a girl we don't like. Maybe, though, you have done something way bigger, something you haven't ever told anybody about.

Lies, disrespect, anger, gossip, pride, sexual behavior—whatever you may be hiding, God's Word has something to say about it:

> The heart is hopelessly dark and deceitful
> a puzzle that no one can figure out.

> But I, GOD, search the heart
> and examine the mind.
> I get to the root of things.
> I treat them as they really are,
> not as they pretend to be
> (Jeremiah 17:9-10 MSG).

God knows your heart. Are you trying to hide the sin in your life? Don't. Jesus knows every single thing about you and me—even the stuff we think we can hide.

Does that scare you? It doesn't have to. The God of the entire universe doesn't just search our hearts; He actually *did* something about them. Jesus' death on the cross wasn't about warm fuzzies. It was about love—the greatest kind of love you and I could ever experience. A love that took God's punishment for all of the sins we've ever committed or ever will.

Jesus' love for us is so amazing. We can no more *earn* His love than we can make the sun shine. God loves us for who we are as His daughters, and we can do nothing to change that.

But Megan, you might be thinking, *you don't know me. I've done too much. I'm too bad for God to forgive*. But that is exactly why Jesus Christ came. The more messed up our lives are, the more we need God's grace.

And that grace is a gift. It's free—not something we can earn. Regardless of what you've done, Jesus took

God's wrath for you. The Bible says that God is ready and waiting not only to forgive us but also to clean up all the nasty, rotten trash in our hearts. God promises to cleanse you from *all* unrighteousness.

No sin is so big that God's forgiveness isn't greater still. So don't try to hide from God. Tell Him all about what you've done. He can't wait to say, *I love you...and I forgive you.*

What's a Girl to Do?

No sin is too big for God. Remember that. Regardless of what the world says, God wants to forgive our sins. If you've got Jesus, you are already forgiven. But if you don't, choose now to believe in Him! Go to "Step One" (page 13) and accept Jesus as Lord and Savior. Receive forgiveness today.

All in with God

Father, thank You for forgiving me of my mistakes. I make them every day, so I'm eternally grateful that Jesus has made a way for me to be reconciled to You. I pray for those who do not know Him. I pray that they won't wait to believe, but that they too may be forgiven. I love You, Lord. You are the best. In Jesus' name, amen.

Drama Queen

*It was for freedom that Christ set us free;
therefore keep standing firm and do not be
subject again to a yoke of slavery.*

GALATIANS 5:1 NASB

Have you ever seen the movie *Confessions of a Teenage Drama Queen*? Very funny! "So much drama, so little time." I know you know what I'm talking about. To this kind of girl, everything's a major production. She loves attention, and the world is her stage. Given the chance to perform, she will shine every time!

A drama queen is a female who talks a lot, cries a lot, and laughs a lot, all in the same five minutes. When she gets to school and notices her fingernail polish is chipped, the whole day is ruined. When the family car is being fixed and she can't go shopping after school, the world is going to end. You get the picture.

I've known some drama queens. They provide great entertainment, but I wonder what is really going on underneath the drama act. *What is she trying to hide? Why doesn't she want us to see the real her?*

Acting takes a lot of work. Constantly having to be something you're not can drain the energy right out of you. You can exhaust yourself by always making sure you're ready to perform at any minute, always watching for everyone's reactions.

Have you ever made a decision based on what you felt in the moment? I have. It's easy to fall into the trap of immediately acting on our feelings, especially when we are hurt. Sure, if we've been genuinely hurt, we'll be angry, jealous, or sad. That's normal. We all feel that way. But our feelings don't have to lead to drama.

We must be careful not to base our decisions on what we're feeling at the moment. Our feelings are important, and we need to pay attention to them. But we also need to stop and think about why we feel the way we do before we act. Otherwise, we set ourselves up for further disappointment and hurt. Immediately acting on our feelings can lead to actions we will later regret deeply—and our sudden choices may even damage those we love most.

God knows we will get riled up. He created us with passions that run deep within our souls, stirring up our emotions. Our job, as followers of Christ, is to ask for His help to control these emotions so we don't make bad decisions in light of our feelings.

God has freed you from the power of sin and the power of your emotions. Praise Jesus! You don't have to be a drama queen—you can be free to be the real you!

What's a Girl to Do?

If you struggle with being an emotional decision maker, remember the freedom we have in Christ. We don't have to be ruled by our emotions. Let's challenge ourselves to make decisions based on our reality in Christ.

All in with God

Father, thank You for Your unending forgiveness! You have made me a passionate young woman, but I don't want to be a drama queen. I trust You to help me identify areas where I struggle. I trust that I can do all things through Christ. Regardless of the results, I know You love me! In Jesus' name, amen.

&$%*#@

*Do not neglect doing good and sharing, for
with such sacrifices God is pleased.*

HEBREWS 13:16 NASB

I was recently riding through Colorado with my family. I must have been the only one who saw a small sign that said Dam Road. As Dad turned onto the road and began to cross a gigantic reservoir, I couldn't resist: "Dam Road is long, isn't it." He turned around and nearly wrecked us. When I showed him the name of the road, we all laughed!

Have you ever heard of No Cussing Clubs? Apparently, a 14-year-old guy named McKay Hatch formed the club when he got tired of all the profanity around him. His family did not allow such language, and McKay got sick of hearing it all the time. He vowed to throw four-letter words out of his own vocabulary, and he encouraged others to do the same.

McKay goes to South Pasadena High School, and his club meets on Wednesdays. They have a website, matching orange shirts, and a hip-hop theme song. Many others have followed his lead. In fact, researchers estimate that nearly 20,000 people have joined similar clubs.

You think McKay doesn't take heat for it? He gets persecuted all of the time for not cussing. Can you believe that? People stop by his club meetings, fire off a few mouth bombs, and leave. He and his family have also been the targets of hate mail and even death threats.

The Bible tells us the tongue is like a flame that can burn an entire forest down if not controlled. It also gives the image of our tongue as the rudder of a giant ship. With the smallest movement of a tiny rudder (or our tongues), an entire boat (or our bodies and minds) can be moved off course (James 3:4-6).

God doesn't want us to give up on speaking, but if you have a bad habit, He can help you overcome it. We all stumble in many ways. But to throw around dirty words is not only trashy and tacky but also ungodly.

Instead, think of all the good we can do with our words and deeds. I'm not talking about being a goody-goody, but about being godly. Practice today saying encouraging words that build people up instead of tear them down. (See Ephesians 4:29.) We are called to a higher standard than the world is. We must be willing to be different, to be like Christ. If you want to be all for God, you need to speak that way.

What's a Girl to Do?

We are not McKay Hatch, but we are daughters of God. With the Holy Spirit living in us, let's challenge ourselves to love others. Let's please God even more with our behavior!

All in with God

Father, I am totally into being Yours. Show me what that means. Guide me into a closer relationship with You. Reveal areas of my life that I need to ditch and replace with the goodness of Christ. I want this, but I can't do it without Your help. Hold my hand, Lord. In Jesus' name, amen.

Who? What? Me?

*Don't fret or worry. Instead of worrying, pray. Let
petitions and praises shape your worries into
prayers, letting God know your concerns. Before
you know it, a sense of God's wholeness, everything
coming together for good, will come and settle
you down. It's wonderful what happens when
Christ displaces worry at the center of your life.*

PHILIPPIANS 4:6-7 MSG

If you've ever been on a blind date, you may relate to
this story—but I really hope not!

My friends had set me up with a really cute guy.
They asked me to join them for a movie and said he
would be there. Oh my! I was completely freaked out!

One problem—they didn't tell him I was coming.
And that's not all. My friends, trying to hook me up,
told the guy I liked him.

When I showed up at the movie theater, the guy
ignored me all night long. Talk about awkward! I began
to worry that he didn't like me or that I had a major
defect that made me unlovable or undesirable. I had

dressed cute and thought I looked nice, but when he ran, I just knew it was my fault. *Do I have a huge zit on my face?* I wondered. *Did my hair frizz? Did I have bad breath or say something stupid?* I became consumed with what went wrong.

I told my mom what had happened. She looked straight at me and asked, "What's wrong with him?"

I told her it was me, not the guy.

She disagreed. "He ran away. That's childish."

Looking back at that night, I now notice how easy it is to become worried when we lose control of a situation, to be anxious when things don't go the way we planned. Is this common? Yes. Is it healthy? Not really.

When we know something is coming, we worry.

When we don't know what is coming, we worry.

And worry causes stress, making us grumpy and unbearable for those we love.

So how do we learn to de-stress our lives? Read today's verse. Pray about *everything*. Give thanks, even when things are bad. Does this mean you won't be anxious at times? Not at all. But it does mean you have a place to take your anxiety. Now read the last sentence in verse 5. The NIV says, "God is near." When we rely on God through prayer, we can trust He is near us whether our circumstances are as minimal as a bad date or as serious as a sick parent, divorce, or even abuse. God is near.

There is no better time than the present to begin a

good habit, and one of the best habits we can cultivate is to push aside anxious thoughts and replace them with prayers of thanksgiving. Listen to the advice of an anonymous quote I came across: "Never trouble trouble till trouble troubles you." We'll give trouble a run for its money when we don't react with worry, but with solid trust in our mighty God!

What's a Girl to Do?

Put Philippians 4:6-7 into action this week. When we begin to worry, let's do what these verses recommend. Pray. Give thanks. And do so repeatedly. Then trust that God will do the rest!

All in with God

Father, this world comes with so much trouble. Anxiety is easy to feel, even on a daily basis. I don't want to be an anxious person. Instead, I want to trust in You, God. Help me to begin to do so by following what Your Word says in Philippians 4. I love You, Lord! In Jesus' name, amen.

A Little More Like Christ

I know how to get along with humble means,
and I also know how to live in prosperity; in
any and every circumstance I have learned the
secret of being filled and going hungry, both of
having abundance and suffering need. I can do
all things through Him who strengthens me.
PHILIPPIANS 4:12-13 NASB

What makes you content? The newest pair of Rocket Dog shoes? Brand-new jeans? What about a contact list full of friends who love to text and just hang out? A boyfriend who really cares and, by the way, looks good?

Let me tell you the story of Ella.

Ella worked as a missionary with pygmies in Africa for 52 years. Mimi, Ella's daughter, wondered how her mother endured the scorching heat and sweltering humidity with such a positive attitude. Then Mimi came across her mother's journal and read this list:

- Never allow yourself to complain about anything—not even the weather.

- Never picture yourself in any other circumstance or someplace else.

- Never compare your lot with another's.

- Never allow yourself to wish this or that had been otherwise.

- Never dwell on tomorrow—remember that [tomorrow] is God's, not ours.

The apostle Paul lived a torturous life after his conversion to Jesus. He suffered shipwrecks, torture, imprisonment, beatings, and more. How did he remain so content? I doubt he had Ella's list of recommended habits, but I do think he and Ella drew their contentment from the same place. Here's the NIV rendering of today's verses: "I know what it is to be in need, and I know what it is to have plenty. I have learned the secret of being content in any and every situation, whether well fed or hungry, whether living in plenty or in want. I can do everything through him who gives me strength" (Philippians 4:12-13).

As a young woman, you may have plenty. Or you may be in want. Generally, our generation is pampered and taken care of more than any before it. I am quite confident that nearly every young woman reading this devotional today has some sort of electronic gadget—an iPod, cell phone, TV, DVD player, or computer.

Without a question, we have been given much. But

with all that we have, I wonder—are we really content? And what about less concrete things? What else do you do to feel satisfied in life? Do you hide behind your good grades? Your sports achievements? Your beautiful voice? Your looks? Do you compare yourself to others, discontent because you don't have what they do?

Contentment in such areas comes easy when life is going well. But how do you do when things get difficult? Where do you go to calm or soothe yourself in stressful times? To feel satisfied and safe again?

Paul and Ella had contentment. They were satisfied in the good times and bad. Not that we should never be discontent—in fact, discontentment can lead to positive change. But when our discontent leads to coveting, stress, and turning to things other than the Lord, it's like telling God we don't trust Him. He wants us to be content in all things, knowing that He is trustworthy. In the good, the bad, and the ugly. Doing so makes us a little more like Paul and Ella. A little more like Christ.

What's a Girl to Do?

Let's try to be content in our own circumstances. Maybe we could drop the minutes on our cell or texts and use the money to sponsor a child or do something else great in Jesus' name. Doing so may help us be content wherever Christ has us.

All in with God

Father, You freely give me good gifts. You provide me with comforts and even most of my wants. Your love is great, and I thank You. Help me to be content regardless of my circumstances and to reach out to those who are in need. In Jesus' name, amen.

People Pleaser

*Whatever you do, do your work heartily, as
for the Lord rather than for men.*
COLOSSIANS 3:23 NASB

The phone rings. You jump out of the shower and
wrap a towel around yourself. *I hope this isn't Shelly
canceling our plans for tonight. I'm so looking forward to
hanging out.*

Running late, you pick up the phone in a flurry.
"Hello?" you say while towel drying your hair.

"Hi. I really need your help tonight..." The voice on
the other end is from a good friend—a friend who often
asks for your help. And because you are so nice and
everyone likes that about you, you never say no.

"Oh?" you answer hesitantly. *What?* Your brain
screams. *I already have plans. This can't be happening.*
"What did you need?"

"I really need someone to babysit my brother and
sister for me," your friend says. "I have to help Holly.
She's really sad and needs to talk."

So tell her she can talk to you while you both *watch your brother and sister,* you think to yourself.

Have you ever been in this situation? What would you do? You so want to be liked, you in no way want to create any waves with anybody, and now here you are with a dilemma. You're in the middle of two friends. Tough call, right?

Look at Jesus' example for a moment. During His ministry, He visited His hometown. Did they throw Him a party? Have a big celebration? Greet Him like a king? No, they did the opposite. These were the people who saw Jesus as a child. They were friends with His normal, sinful family. They wondered how He could be the promised Messiah. After all, He was the son of Joseph—the local carpenter.

Knowing who He was, that He *was* the promised one, allowed Jesus to make decisions accordingly— regardless of what others thought, regardless of what they believed. Jesus boldly proclaimed who He was and what He stood for. Those in His own hometown got mad, even threatening to throw Him off a cliff. So what did Jesus do? He made His way through the angry crowd and left. Jesus was going to preach elsewhere.

Jesus was *not* a people pleaser. He was a God pleaser. He knew not only who He was but also whose He was.

I don't know about you, but this is hard for me. I want to make others happy. I often spend so much time trying to please people that sometimes I lose sight of myself. It can leave me feeling angry at somebody—usually myself.

We should do good to all, as we have a chance (Galatians 6:10). But something is wrong if you become miserable and begin to lose your own identity. Once you discover who you are—and whose you are—you no longer have to seek other people's approval, just God's (Galatians 1:10).

What's a Girl to Do?

Let's make an effort this week to please God first. You may want to do something for Him that others won't see (so they won't be able to praise you). Then you can bask in the knowledge that God is happy with your good choice!

All in with God

Father, thank You for loving me! I enjoy learning about You and what You are like. Give me wisdom so I can deal kindly with others. Help me to always do Your good, pleasing, and perfect will. In Jesus' name, amen.

Tomorrow

*Now listen, you who say, "Today or tomorrow we will go
to this or that city, spend a year there, carry on business
and make money." Why, you do not even know what
will happen tomorrow...Instead, you ought to say, "If
it is the Lord's will, we will live and do this or that." As
it is, you boast and brag. All such boasting is evil.*

JAMES 4:13-16

My mom loves lists. If we're throwing a party, she
has lists of people, food, expenses, you name it.
If we go grocery shopping, she has a list. If we go on
vacation, she has a list. If she tells dad to do something,
she gives him a list (which he always either loses or
ignores). My mom loves to be organized and in control.

Do you? Most of us do. We have short-term and
long-term goals. And this is great. But what happens
when something unexpected comes along, like a sick-
ness? Or maybe a friend or family member calls in need.
Or maybe you don't make the team.

I've struggled with this time and again. Many times,
I want things my way. But when things don't go my way

and I remain inflexible, I get irritable and unpleasant to be around. Listen to today's verse in The Message:

> Now I have a word for you who brashly announce, "Today—at the latest, tomorrow—we're off to such and such city for the year. We're going to start a business and make a lot of money." You don't know the first thing about tomorrow. You're nothing but a wisp of fog, catching a brief bit of sun before disappearing. Instead, make it a habit to say, "If the Master wills it, and we're still alive, we'll do this or that."

If I had to guess, I would say James was a pretty straightforward guy. He cut to the chase and laid it all out on the table for everyone to see. Maybe he had heard Christians talk as if they ran their lives themselves and he wanted to help them understand that God is the one who really guides our steps. (See Proverbs 16:9.)

Jesus preached a similar message. "Do not worry about tomorrow, for tomorrow will worry about itself. Each day has enough trouble of its own" (Matthew 6:33-34).

I'm not advocating giving up your planner. I'm suggesting that we hold our plans loosely, acknowledge God's overall control, surrender to do His will above all, and sit back and see what happens. It may not be what we expected or desired. My guess is it will be better in the end than anything *we* could have penciled down!

What's a Girl to Do?

Most of us have some kind of planner, BlackBerry, or iPhone that helps us plan our days, weeks, and months. As I said, we don't have to trash them. We just need to have the attitude that God is really in control. We are to trust in Him. Let's do it!

All in with God

Father, I love You! No one is more capable to order my life than You are. You may plan things I do not expect, but I trust in Your goodness. Help me to keep an attitude like Christ's. I give it to You, Lord. Be my personal organizer. In Jesus' name, amen.

Humble

Do you want to stand out? Then step down. Be a servant. If you puff yourself up, you'll get the wind knocked out of you. But if you're content to simply be yourself, your life will count for plenty.
MATTHEW 23:12 MSG

Remember *Spider-Man 3*? The gorgeous redheaded Kirsten Dunst is Spider-Man's girl. The totally cute Tobey Maguire is Spider-Man. However, in this particular movie, Spider-Man is not so cute. The underlying theme is a battle between his good nature (servanthood and love) and evil nature (pride and a hunger for power).

Spider-Man's pride causes him to lose touch with those who matter most to him. As a result, his most important relationships break, leaving him desperate and alone. In his love of power, he neglects his most cherished relationships.

Do you want to stand out for Christ? Do you want to be used in great ways for His glory? Then you must learn the meaning of humility.

I'm not saying we all need to be doormats. Being humble doesn't mean being quiet or weak. It simply means we realize that without God, we would be nothing. A humble person is always aware of who He is (God) and who we are (God's servants). Living this way, we will be content, and our life can really count for God.

Pride is just about the opposite. A prideful girl doesn't think she needs to compare herself to anyone because no one would measure up to her. If she does make comparisons, she looks down on others as inferior to her. Pride is ultimately a result of selfishness. When we only focus on ourselves and forget that we are created by the Creator, we become prideful about what we think we have achieved. We think it is all of our own doing and not blessing from God.

Setting the perfect example, Jesus humbly bore the sins of the world in total humility. He was the King of kings, yet He humbled Himself enough to come to our world as a human. Even more, He was willing to die the most humiliating death imaginable. Now *that's* true love, sacrifice, and humility!

The Bible warns us to humble ourselves. I think we have no other choice. Either we humble ourselves or God and others will humble us. Pride will humiliate you, but humility will honor you. To be all in for God is to practice humility.

What's a Girl to Do?

Sometimes the most humble act is to allow an honor to pass over us. I have no idea what activities you are pursuing or whether you are prideful or humble. Let's pray that God would show us how to act out true humility this week in service to others for His glory!

All in with God

Father, thank You for Your example of humility in Jesus. The world is so full of pride that I easily forget I am not of the world and don't have to be like it. Through the power of the Holy Spirit, please give me a humble heart. In Jesus' name, amen.

True Love

*"YOU SHALL LOVE THE LORD YOUR GOD
WITH ALL YOUR HEART, AND WITH ALL
YOUR SOUL, AND WITH ALL YOUR MIND."*
This is the great and foremost commandment.

Matthew 22:37-38 nasb

We are a generation and a nation that likes to indulge ourselves. Whatever catches our attention on television, in magazines, or through other media sources soon becomes our obsession. We have to have that new haircut to match Taylor Swift's, the shoes like Miley Cyrus's, or the new music by Hilary Duff. Look at all the money Americans spend on advertising—billions! And it's all put into enticing us to desire or *love* a product.

It's easy to say we *love* our new hoodie or cute toe ring we bought at Target. But what are we really saying? Not that we *love* the item we bought, but that we love how it makes us feel and look. We want to be noticed, and we easily become infatuated with *loving* things because they make us feel and look lovely.

That may be twisted and hard to understand, but what I'm trying to get across is this: We absolutely *must* keep love real. As girls who are all in for God, we know whom Jesus calls us to love. Jesus explains that we should love the Lord our God first. Then we should love our neighbor.

God gives us the capacity to love not only Him but also those around us. The tricky part is learning how to love Him first. In my opinion, we begin to love God first when we spend time with Him. We pray, read the Bible, and worship and praise His name. As we do, our love for God grows. And soon, He is first in our lives.

I think one of the greatest parts about loving God first is that our eyes are opened. We can't help but see and know His love for all of mankind. We realize more than ever how much Jesus loved us.

Whom and what do you love? Where and with whom do you spend most of your time? Love is powerful, and it is meant for good. Love God and love people—that is being all in for God!

What's a Girl to Do?

Together, let's commit to seek God first by talking with Him daily, trusting in His faithfulness, reading His Word, worshipping Him, and obeying His commands. Love God and love others!

All in with God

Father, I so want You to be my first love. I want to love You with all my heart, soul, and mind, Lord. That is the ultimate—to be in an intimate relationship with You, my God who created me with love and for love! In Jesus' name, amen.

Where Do We Go from Here?

Thanks for joining me on this journey of being all in for God!

Continuing along this path will take commitment. Be sure to find other Christian books and devotionals to supplement your Bible reading. Know of my love and prayers for you. Never quit and never compromise. God really loves you and has a dream for your life. Press in close to Him, and I know you will be free to live it out every day!

Warmly,

MORE GREAT DEVOTIONALS FROM
HARVEST HOUSE PUBLISHERS

One Minute with God

Hope Lyda, author of the popular One–Minute Prayers series (more than 420,000 copies sold) now offers more moments of encouragement, reflection, and inspiration in this gathering of devotions, verses, and prayers designed for the needs of busy readers. Each meditation will bring readers

- refreshment for life's journey
- guidance in daily concerns
- connection and communion with God
- perspective to brighten a moment
- peace during uncertain times

With a fresh observational, simple style, these engaging devotions turn the reader's heart, mind, and focus toward the presence of God's love and the amazing miracle of faith lived out each day.

A Young Woman After God's Own Heart—
A Devotional

Elizabeth George shares the best of her books *A Young Woman After God's Own Heart, A Young Woman's Call to Prayer,* and *A Young Woman's Walk with God.* You'll enjoy these short, dynamic, practical messages that build good habits, cultivate can-do attitudes, and fan the flames of passion for God.

Walking with the Women of the Bible

You'll be intrigued and inspired as you become friends with Eve, Deborah, Leah, Mary, and other biblical women. The devotions from Elizabeth George highlight the way God reached out to these women and changed their lives...and He will do the same for you, helping you handle your situations and grow spiritually.

To learn more about Harvest House books and
to read sample chapters, log on to our website:

www.harvesthousepublishers.com

HARVEST HOUSE PUBLISHERS
EUGENE, OREGON